To Harold Weaver,

When we talked about completing "the book," I never thought it would be this boo...t's finish the original in ...

Best,

Pat Regan

The financial reality of
pension funding under ERISA

The financial reality of pension funding under ERISA

Jack L. Treynor
Financial Analysts Journal

Patrick J. Regan
BEA Associates, Inc.

William W. Priest, Jr.
BEA Associates, Inc.

DOW JONES-IRWIN Homewood, Illinois 60430

First Printing, July 1976

ISBN 0-87094-124-0
Library of Congress Catalog Card No. 76-17352
Printed in the United States of America

TO

BETSY, KATHY, AND NANCY

Preface

This book deals with the financial reality of pension funding under the Employee Retirement Income Security Act (ERISA). Because ERISA was designed primarily from legal and actuarial perspectives, little of value has been written about the financial implications of the law. However, bankers, money managers, security analysts, bond rating agencies, and particularly corporate executives must recognize that ERISA alters the capital structure of every firm that has an unfunded vested pension liability and will affect capital allocation throughout our economy.

From a foundation of modern capital markets theory and experience in advising and managing pension funds, the authors have developed an approach for determining the true impact of pension costs and unfunded liabilities on individual companies. In this book, we attempt to define the real issues of pension management under ERISA, reveal what is at stake for the plan sponsors and their creditors, discuss provisions of ERISA that are likely to be revised, offer suggestions for reasonably administering the Pension Benefit Guarantee Corporation, and outline tactics for employers and fund managers to deal effectively with the realities discussed in the book.

ACKNOWLEDGMENTS

We are indebted to many teachers and professional investors but no one has had a greater impact upon the organization of this book or its arguments than Joseph H. Spigelman, Director for Research of BEA Associates. His contributions extend over two years in time and include hundreds of pages of written material, much of which has been used as source material for this book. Although we often failed to satisfy his incisive criticisms, they have been a challenge and an example for us all.

We would also like to express our appreciation to Marianne Lenczowski and Kathi Gefers for their untiring assistance in the preparation of this manuscript.

Needless to say, none of the people who were so generous with their help are in any way responsible for the ideas and conclusions expressed in this book.

June 1976   **Jack L. Treynor**
                                                   Patrick J. Regan
                                                   William W. Priest, Jr.

Contents

Introduction

When the Employee Retirement Income Security Act (ERISA) was signed by President Ford on Labor Day 1974, pensions were converted from gratuities to corporate liabilities enforceable at law. Whereas the legal claim of pension beneficiaries was formerly limited to pension assets, ERISA extended it to include corporate assets, up to 30 percent of net worth. In the event of a plan termination, which need not involve the liquidation of the company, such claims assume the status of a federal tax lien and rank prior to unsecured claims of corporate creditors. In effect, because it places creditors in a potentially subordinate position, ERISA alters the capital structure of every firm that has an unfunded vested pension liability.

Pensions are now an integral part of corporate planning and decision making. For example, in August of 1975 a Kennecott Copper subsidiary, Chase Brass and Copper, decided to permanently close a plant and phase out its business in condenser tubes and alloy wire. The estimated after-tax charge to Kennecott was $15.5 million, of which $13 million related to an unfunded pension liability.

Those responsible for corporate or pension planning have to address three principal issues:

1. *What is the real liability of the plan-sponsoring company?* What are the pension claims worth, and how is the present value affected by the actuary's discounting techniques? On the asset side, how can the liquidity and risk level of the portfolio be controlled to meet plan objectives? To what extent is portfolio risk borne by the company, its creditors, the plan beneficiaries, and the Pension Benefit Guarantee Corporation?
2. *What are the financial implications of ERISA?* What will be the reaction of bankers and other creditors who are in a po-

1

tentially subordinate position? Will bond ratings be affected by large unfunded pension liabilities?

3. *Will ERISA work?* In the aggregate, what are the real pension risks? Is contingent liability insurance a viable concept? Can ERISA be made to work? How will future changes in the law affect employees?

As the title implies, our principal concern is the *financial reality* of pension funds. The 200 pages of rules and exceptions to rules is the legal reality of ERISA. The standard mortality tables, turnover figures, and historical rate of return studies constitute the actuarial reality. True to form, the accountants are still debating the accounting reality. But the marketplace dictates financial reality. As Clive Granger and Oskar Morgenstern stated in their book *Predictability of Stock Market Prices,* "A thing, no matter what it be, is worth only what someone else will pay for it. . . . Value depends entirely on expectations."[1] It is our contention that ERISA will alter the expectations of investors, bankers, creditors, and employees. Furthermore, the market price of the company's stock and bonds, and hence its ability to raise capital, will reflect this financial reality, regardless of the figures reported by the firm's actuaries and accountants.

---

[1] Clive Granger and Oskar Morgenstern, *Predictability of Stock Market Prices* (Lexington, Mass.: Heath Lexington Books, 1970).

Part 1

Death of the gold watch concept

Chapter 1

Why ERISA now?

THE CATCH IN THE PROMISE

Every generation or so, Congress passes a landmark piece of legislation that alters the social, political, and economic fabric of American life. The Social Security Act of 1935 established government old-age and disability pensions. The Employment Act of 1946 declared that it was the federal government's responsibility and policy to "promote maximum employment, production and purchasing power." In keeping with this tradition, the Employee Retirement Income Security Act (ERISA) promises to be the landmark legislation of the 1970s.

When ERISA was signed in 1974, the U.S. private pension system had been in existence for nearly a century. By 1950, 75 years after the American Express Company established the first formalized pension plan in the United States, 9.8 million Americans were covered by private pension plans and 450,000 retirees were collecting $370 million in annual benefits. Between 1950 and 1973, the number of people covered rose threefold to over 30 million, the number of retirees collecting benefits rose thirteenfold to 6 million, pension assets rose fifteenfold to $180 billion, and benefit payments rose thirtyfold to $11.4 billion a year.[1]

Such statistics testified to the success of the private pension system. But government researchers had some equally impressive figures of a different sort. In April of 1972, the Bureau of the Census conducted a study for the Departments of Treasury, Labor, and

---

[1] "Pension and Retirement Plans in the United States," *The Tally of Life Insurance Statistics* (New York: Institute of Life Insurance, February 1975).

Health, Education and Welfare.[2] The survey revealed that only half of the full-time workers in private industry were covered by private pension or profit sharing plans. Furthermore, only one third of those covered had vested claims to benefits (therefore inalienable even if an employee leaves the plan-sponsoring company). Perhaps most surprising, only half of the employees over 50 years of age and with 20 or more years of service were vested. Other studies have shown that through 1974, little more than one third of those Americans who had, at one time or another in their work histories, been covered by pension plans had actually received any benefits upon retirement.[3]

The stringent vesting and participation standards imposed by some companies were publicized in the controversial 1972 NBC television documentary, "Pensions, the Broken Promise," and during the congressional hearings on pensions that extended over many years. One man testified that although he had worked at the same job for a particular company for 24 years before being fired, he did not qualify for a pension because, under the company's plan, benefits did not vest until after 25 years of continuous service. Another man put in nearly 40 years with one company, but because he had worked at different plants and divisions, each of which had its own retirement plan, he did not qualify for a pension; he had not accumulated enough continuous service under any one plan. In a related case, a man who had worked a total of 30 years for one company, did not qualify for benefits because he had been laid off a few times during that three-decade span. Each layoff was treated as a disqualifying "break in service."

Those fortunate enough to qualify for pensions had no assurance that there would be sufficient funds to cover their retirement benefits. In theory, under a noncontributory plan the employer was to transfer enough money every year to the pension fund to provide for estimated retirement benefits. But as new labor contracts were negotiated and benefits were improved, unfunded past-service costs increased. Although some companies amortized those costs over

---

[2] "Coverage and Vesting of Full-Time Employees under Private Retirement Plans: Findings from the April 1972 Survey," *Bureau of Labor Statistics, Report No. 423,* September 1973.

[3] Ralph Nader and Kate Blackwell, *You and Your Pension* (New York: Grossman Publishers, 1973).

periods of 10 to 40 years, there was no legal requirement to do so. Even with seemingly proper funding, there was no guarantee that the gap between pension assets and vested liabilities would be reduced. As William F. Marples stated in *Actuarial Aspects of Pension Security*, "The peculiar difficulty in judging the condition of a pension plan is that its assets may be growing even as it is becoming more and more insolvent actuarially, and the reason is that the full measure of its outgo may take many years to develop."[4]

In addition to inadequate funding, a few pension plans suffered as a result of the dishonesty, incompetence, or irresponsibility of those charged with administering the funds. In a notorious case, that of the International Brotherhood of Teamsters, a substantial portion of the pension assets was diverted to the financial benefit of plan trustees and their associates. Other plans ignored the principle of diversification and concentrated the pension assets in the securities of local firms or of the plan-sponsoring company itself, strategies which proved extremely risky when the local economy or the financial condition of the company deteriorated and the value of the shares plummeted.

In the great majority of cases, the pension fund risks were borne by the pension beneficiaries, while the rewards from superior portfolio performance accrued to the plan-sponsoring company. Pension claimants ordinarily gained nothing from successful risk taking because their benefits were usually defined independently of the condition of the fund from which the pensions were to be paid. On the other hand, portfolio appreciation could enable the sponsoring company to reduce its annual contribution, or at least increase it at a lesser rate than would otherwise have been necessary. If the risky investments did not work out and the company was unwilling or unable to boost its contribution to make up the deficiency, the loss was borne by the pension claimants, who stood to forfeit some or all of the benefits to which they were entitled. Hence, for the plan-sponsoring company, it was clearly a "heads, I win, tails, you lose" situation. This was consistent with the historical view of a pension as a gratuity, but inconsistent with the position which evolved under ERISA.[5]

---

[4] William F. Marples, *Actuarial Aspects of Pension Security* (Homewood, Ill.: Richard D. Irwin, Inc., 1965).

[5] See Appendix A for an account of the legal evolution of pension rights.

ERISA CLOSES THE GAP

The architects of ERISA sought to correct these and related flaws of the U.S. private pension system. The new law does not require the establishment of a pension plan, but it does prescribe minimum standards for existing and future plans. The standards were chiefly designed to secure the rights of pension participants and to assure adequate funding of the pension plans that define the rights.

Securing rights to pensions

It was not uncommon for companies to severely restrict participation in their pension plans. Many would exclude younger workers, especially those under the age of 30, and employees with less than five, ten, or more years of service. Another common practice was to exclude workers hired relatively late in life, even those no more than 45 years old.

Under the new law, employees who are at least 25 years old and have completed one year of service must be covered by the pension plan. In addition, a worker who has completed three years of service must be given credit for that service when he or she turns 25. To protect older workers who change jobs, the act permits a defined benefit plan to exclude only those employees hired within five years of normal retirement age. Thus, full-time employees who were between the ages of 24 and 60 when starting with the firm and who have completed at least one year of service should be participating in the company pension plan, if there is one.

Participation does not guarantee that an individual will actually collect a pension. Employees have to reach a certain age or complete a certain period of service before their pension benefits become "vested," so assuring their right to receive them upon retirement whether or not they remain with the company. Most of the tragic stories told by witnesses at the congressional hearings involved pension plans with overly stringent vesting provisions.

To insure that employees with many years of service will not forfeit their pensions, the act requires companies to adopt one of three vesting methods as a minimum standard.[6] In no case will a worker be less than 50 percent vested after ten years of service.

Prior to the act, some plans violated the spirit of vesting by "backloading" the benefits and accruing a low rate of benefits during

---

[6] See Appendix B for the major provisions of ERISA.

an employee's early years of service and a higher rate during his or her later years. For example, a plan might credit a monthly pension benefit of $2 for each year of service up to age 60, and $20 for each year of service from ages 60 to 65. Under such a plan, a worker in his or her late fifties who was fired might be fully vested but because of backloading the worker's benefits would be miniscule. To correct the abuses of backloading, ERISA mandates the choice of one of three rules, all intended to limit differences in the rates at which claims to pension benefits may accrue at different periods in an employee's service.

Another important feature of the act is that vested benefits are nonforfeitable. Companies will no longer be able to withhold vested benefits from participants who violate "competitive activity" clauses.

Such clauses were often included in retirement contracts to prevent valuable employees from leaving the company to set up their own operation or to work for a competitor. If they did so, they automatically forfeited all pension benefits, including their vested rights. But under ERISA, vested benefits are nonforfeitable, even if an employee violates a competitive activity agreement or is convicted of criminal conduct.

Loopholes in vesting are plugged by "break-in-service" rules. Prior to the act, most plans required a number of years of *continuous* service for an employee to become vested. Blue-collar workers who were subject to periodic layoffs and women who, because of marriage and childbearing, temporarily quit or switched to part-time work were the principal victims of the "break-in-service" loopholes. Under ERISA, breaks in service can only occur if employees work less than 500 hours a year. If breaks occur before employees are vested, they can return to the company, mend the break, and pick up where they left off in years of service, so long as their absence was less than the length of their prior service.

Finally, to assure that vested benefits are paid in the event that an underfunded plan terminates, the Pension Benefit Guaranty Corporation (PBGC), a government agency set up by ERISA, guarantees payment of vested benefits (within limits spelled out in Appendix B).

The funding requirements of ERISA

Through funding, annual pension contributions are translated into pension assets. The policy of most large corporations is to "fund pension costs as accrued." In layman's terms, this means that the typical firm makes an annual cash contribution to its pension fund in an amount equal to the "pension expense" it charged against income in its audited financial statements.

The size of a firm's annual pension expense and its liability for unfunded past service costs (if any) can vary dramatically, depending on the method of funding and the actuarial assumptions selected. Before ERISA, companies were only required to fund their normal service costs (i.e., those attributed to benefit credits gained for the current year's service) and the interest on their unfunded past-service costs (those assigned to prior years of service); though in practice most large corporations amortized their unfunded pension liabilities over periods of 30 to 40 years. The new law requires that the unfunded liabilities as of January 1, 1974, be amortized over a maximum period of 40 years, while initial past-service costs of new plans and increases in the unfunded past-service costs of existing plans must be amortized over a period of 30 years or less.

The unfunded pension liability itself is a function of two variables, both of which can be strongly affected by the decisions of an actuary—the valuation of the pension fund assets and the present value of the pension benefits. Disregarding corporate contributions, the realizable value of pension fund assets rise and fall with the stock and bond markets. However, for actuarial valuation purposes, less than one out of four major firms uses market value.[7] Most of them value the pension assets at cost or adjusted cost, which reflects a portion of any unrealized appreciation in a single year. Being free to recognize or not recognize unrealized appreciation, many companies were able to manage their annual contributions, and, hence, their reported earnings.

To prevent such arbitrary decisions, the act specifies how "experience" gains and losses, most of which result from the performance of the pension fund portfolio, must be handled. Companies will have to determine their actuarial gains and losses at least once every three years, and such gains or losses must be amortized over a 15-year period from the time they are determined. With the exception of bonds, which can be valued at cost, assets will be valued at market. Hence, corporate treasurers will have to pay more attention to the fluctuations of their pension fund portfolios. If the three-year

---

[7] The Conference Board, *Financial Management of Company Pension Plans* (New York, 1973).

determination period happened to occur during a bear market, the company would have to amortize the loss and step up its annual pension contribution, penalizing pretax profits in the process.

In addition to its impact on asset valuation, ERISA limits the ability of the actuary to control the liability side of the pension fund. The pension liability is equal to the present value of retirement benefits owed, and the actuary plays a key role in helping the company estimate the magnitude of the variables in the present-value model, including employee turnover, disability and mortality figures, normal retirement age, the impact of inflation on salary scales, the length of service and income level at retirement, the degree to which social security benefits will supplement the pension payments and, most important, the expected return on the pension fund portfolio.

Obviously, with so many variables, it is difficult to compare the pension costs and unfunded liabilities of different plans. But ERISA introduces an element of uniformity, since the actuarial assumptions will have to be certified as "reasonable" by a registered actuary, and the report will have to be signed by a certified public accountant.

Hence, the funding provisions of the act require companies to identify and amortize their unfunded past-service costs, to recognize and systematically amortize experience gains and losses, and to have their actuarial assumptions certified as "reasonable." The law has some teeth in it in that companies that fail to meet the minimum funding standards will be subject to a 5 percent excise tax on the accumulated deficiency and a 100 percent excise tax if the deficiency is not corrected promptly. The company may qualify as a hardship case and obtain a year-by-year waiver of the funding standards, but the amount will have to be made up at later date.

Questions of liability and risk

In addition to its eligibility, vesting, and funding provisions, ERISA covers two other major issues: who will fulfill the pension obligations of terminated plans and who may be held liable for poor investment decisions? Unfortunately, these are financial questions and the legal arguments and answers outlined in ERISA are confusing and contradictory.

Consider the law's provisions governing plan termination. Should a pension plan be terminated, whether voluntarily or involuntarily, the PBGC will step in to pay guaranteed benefits. Involuntary termination (which need not involve bankruptcy or liquidation of a plan sponsor) can occur when a company fails to meet ERISA's funding standards, is unable to pay benefits falling due, or when company action or circumstances make it likely that the Guaranty Corporation's liability for paying guaranteed benefits would tend to "increase unreasonably" unless the plan is terminated. The PBGC will pay guaranteed benefits, using first the assets accumulated under the terminated plan. Should the assets, when converted to cash, prove inadequate, the Guaranty Corporation can hold the company liable for 100 percent of the underfunding of guaranteed benefits under the terminated plan and has the power to attach a lien to corporate assets, equivalent to as much as 30 percent of the company's net worth in order to discharge this liability. The lien would have the same priority as a federal tax lien and would accordingly be senior to debentures, bank loans, and the claims of other corporate creditors. Thus the law attempts to make the pension-sponsoring company itself—and not merely the pension funds it has established—fully responsible and liable for fulfilling the pension claims it has created, and fully subject also to the risks it may have taken with pension assets.

There is, however, a significant loophole in the law. A seemingly minor provision of ERISA, Section 4023, provides that companies will be able to insure themselves against contingent liabilities (i.e., the PBGC lien, up to 30 percent of net worth, that could result if the plan was terminated and pension assets were inadequate to meet the guaranteed benefits) through the PBGC or by private insurance carriers. The act, as it now reads, requires that the system of contingent liability insurance become operative no later than September 1977.[8]

Thus, in one section of the law, ERISA makes pension-sponsoring companies fully liable for their pension promises; but in another section, it furnishes them the means of escaping such liability. This contradiction in the law raises issues that will be a major concern throughout the book. In sum, Congress sought to make pension

---

[8] Section 4023 of ERISA calls for the Pension Benefit Guarantee Corporation to offer contingent liability insurance by September 1977. However, in June 1975, Congressmen Dent and Erlenborn introduced a bill, H. R. 7597, that would have pushed the date up to September 1975.

promises real both to the pension participant and the pension-sponsoring company. Plan participation, vesting, and funding standards were the principal methods used to achieve this objective. Furthermore, a government agency, the PBGC, was created to ensure that the employee received benefits due in the event of a plan termination. The law also authorized this agency to lay claim to corporate assets in order to offset, in whole or in part, its outlays to beneficiaries.

Perhaps as a way to ease the burden of larger pension liabilities resulting from the enactment of this law, Congress provided a means by which employers could insure their contingent liability. Implementation of this provision of ERISA can place the employer corporation in the same position as prior to ERISA but the PBGC would bear the risk of an unsuccessful funding program rather than the employee.

With the hardening of the pension liability, what is the magnitude of the pension burden and related liabilities? How do these magnitudes relate to the size and structure of the sponsoring corporations? This perspective is the subject of the next two chapters.

Chapter 2

Funding the pension burden—The conventional view

After ERISA became law, security analysts, bankers, credit rating agencies, and investors turned their attention to the annual pension costs and unfunded liabilities of the companies in which they had an interest. What they discovered was that pension funding is a complex subject, with dozens of variables, little uniformity, and inadequate disclosure. The pension expense and unfunded liability figures of different companies are often not comparable because the companies may be using different funding methods, actuarial assumptions, eligibility standards, and vesting provisions. Despite these difficulties, one of your authors gathered six years of pension data on 40 major corporations and summarized the results in a series of research reports for Merrill Lynch, Pierce, Fenner & Smith, Inc.[1] This chapter is based largely on those surveys and contains summary statistics relating to the size and growth of pension costs for a cross section of American industry. We caution that the figures were computed by conventional actuarial and accounting techniques. In later chapters, we will suggest an unconventional but more relevant framework for the examination of the pension burden.

---

[1] The 1973 figures and the 1969–73 annual growth rates in this chapter were taken from Patrick J. Regan, "Pension Costs and Unfunded Liabilities—A Special Report," Merrill Lynch, Pierce, Fenner & Smith, Inc., October 2, 1974. The 1974 figures were taken from Jack L. Treynor and Patrick J. Regan, "Valuing Corporations with Unfunded Pension Liabilities," a paper presented before the Institute for Quantitative Research in Finance, May 4, 1975.

DETERMINING THE LEVEL OF PENSION CONTRIBUTIONS

In conventional analysis, a company's "pension expense" is roughly equivalent to its annual pension contributions.[2] In 1973, the year before ERISA became law, the sum of $21.7 billion was paid into private pension and retirement plans, and employers contributed over 90 percent of the total. The plans dispensed $11.4 billion to retirees, and the other $10.3 billion was added to pension fund assets.[3] At the end of 1974, such assets amounted to $193 billion on a cost basis, with approximately 31 percent held by insured plans and 69 percent held by noninsured pension funds.[4]

Although some companies have a single pension plan and others have as many plans as they have subsidiaries, the typical large corporation has two plans, one for the salaried employees and one for the hourly employees. In addition, a few industries have "multiemployer" plans, which are negotiated and administered by a labor union and numerous employer companies.

Regardless of the type or number of plans, nearly all companies list a single pension expense figure in their annual reports. But few firms indicate how they compute the pension expense.

The annual pension expense figure and the size of the liability for unfunded past-service costs will be different under different funding methods. Of the five principal funding methods, three (the unit credit, entry age normal, and attained age normal methods) involve a liability for unfunded past-service costs.[5] Under those methods, the pension expense figure is composed of two parts—the

---

[2] The pension contribution is the amount the company turns over to the plan trustees, whereas the pension expense is the amount it charges to the current period's income. In a given year, a company might charge more to income than it actually contributes, in which case the difference is accrued but not funded. Of course, it is posssible for the amount funded to exceed the amount accrued. The policy of most companies is to fund pension costs as they are accrued.

[3] "Pension and Retirement Plans in the United States," *The Tally of Life Insurance Statistics* (New York: Institute of Life Insurance, February 1975).

[4] Securities and Exchange Commission, "Private Noninsured Pension Funds, 1974," *SEC Statistical Bulletin*, April 1975. In the case of an insured plan, the company pays an annual premium or a lump sum to an insurance company instead of making a contribution to its pension fund. In turn, the insurance company underwrites the retirement benefits by selling an annuity or by guaranteeing a fixed investment return for a specified period of time, usually five to ten years. Under a noninsured or self-insured plan, the investment return is open-ended, as the company's annual pension contribution is placed into a trust, the assets of which are generally invested in stocks, bonds, mortgages, and real estate.

[5] See Appendix C for a description of the principal actuarial funding methods.

"normal service" costs incurred during the year and the amortization of the unfunded past-service costs, generally over a period of 30 or 40 years. Under the other two methods (the aggregate and the individual level premium methods) unfunded past-service costs are not separately identified but are amortized over the remaining working lives assumed for the employees and are included with normal service costs. Because the remaining working lives of employees are generally much less than 30 or 40 years, the pension expense computed under those methods is greater than it would be under one of the other three methods in the early years of the plan. But ultimately, a specified amount of money must be in the fund to pay the benefits at retirement, so the difference in methods is essentially a matter of timing. Actuaries sometimes use the analogy of life insurance policy premiums to explain the difference in funding methods. If an individual bought a renewable term insurance policy, the premiums would be very low initially but would rise as the individual ages and might well become prohibitively large in the final years of normal life expectancy. On the other hand, if a whole life policy is purchased, the premiums would be relatively high in the early years but would remain fixed. So, too, a company using the aggregate method would report a higher pension expense in the early years of a plan than it would under the unit credit method (see Figure 2–1).[6]

While the funding method affects the timing of the pension costs, the total amount of funds that must be accumulated is a function of the actuarial assumptions. In order to estimate the amount of benefits that the plan will have to pay out in future years, the plan administrators have to estimate (a) how many employees will remain with the company until retirement age or leave with vested benefits; (b) what the normal retirement age will be, the benefits formula, and the degree to which benefits will be reduced for those who take early retirement; (c) the length of service and income at retirement; (d) the length of time the employee will live beyond retirement; and (e) the expected level of social security payments, inflation, and other factors. The estimates and the tables and the assumptions on which they are based can differ widely. Among companies whose assumptions we have examined, mortality tables are as outdated as the 1937 Group Annuity table and as recent as a

---

[6] The chart in Figure 2–1 was taken from Robert A. Davidow, *Accounting for Pension Plan Costs* (Lehman Brothers, Inc., March 6, 1975).

1970 table; retirement ages range from 61 to 65, and salary scales or cost-of-living factors range from 0 to 8½ percent per annum. Whatever the estimates, they can be entered into a computer model in order to determine how much money must be set aside each year to accumulate the necessary fund.

The money to fund a noncontributory plan will come from two sources—the pension contributions of the employer and the investment returns generated by the assets in the pension fund. The ex-

FIGURE 2–1

Funding patterns

Pension contribution

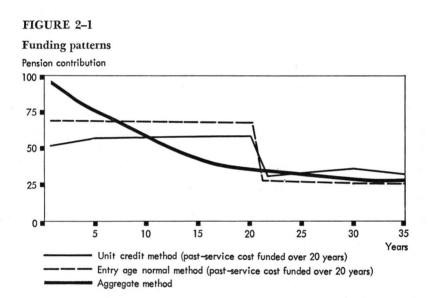

——————— Unit credit method (past–service cost funded over 20 years)
– – – – – Entry age normal method (past–service cost funded over 20 years)
▬▬▬▬▬ Aggregate method

pected return on invested assets, which is also known as the "interest rate assumption," is the key actuarial assumption. The higher the expected investment return, the smaller the unfunded pension liability and the lower the required company contribution. With the other assumptions held constant, a 1 percent increase in the interest rate assumption allows for an increase in pension benefits or a decrease in pension contributions of 16 percent to 30 percent.

In the late 1960s companies concluded that their 3 percent to 4 percent interest rate assumptions were very conservative, since AAA-rated bonds offered 7 percent returns and the stock market had been posting 15-percent-plus annual returns for nearly two decades. Hence, it was not surprising that many companies began boosting their yield assumptions from the 3 percent to 4 percent range to the current 5 percent to 6 percent level. For example, in 1973 The Conference Board studied the pension plans of 117 major corporations and found that 80 of the firms had increased their interest rate assumptions between 1969 and 1972. The results ranged from as low as 3½ percent to a high of 8 percent.[7] Similarly, the Merrill Lynch survey showed that 22 of the 40 companies examined increased their yield assumptions between 1968 and 1974, including 8 that raised their assumptions two or three times during the seven-year period.[8] Corporations usually consult their actuaries before they enter labor contract negotiations, so that they will have estimates of the cost of possible benefit increases. Because the actuarial assumptions are reexamined at the same time, it is not surprising that changes tend to coincide with the signing of new labor contracts to "ease" the burden imposed by benefit improvements.

Another method commonly employed to hold pension expenses in check was to revalue pension assets by taking unrealized appreciation into account. For example, on August 10, 1972, when benefits under a new labor contract became effective, U.S. Steel started giving additional recognition to the unrealized appreciation in its $2 billion pension fund portfolio. This change enabled the company to reduce its pension expense by one third, from $137 million to $90 million, with the $47 million savings going directly into 1973 pretax earnings.

However, the impact of such changes is not always spelled out. The reduction in pension expense from the yield increase often equals the benefit increase so that, in accounting terminology, the net change is "immaterial." Thus, in 1971 a major chemical company increased its actuarial interest rate assumption from 4 percent to 5.5 percent, adopted a new pension asset valuation formula, reduced the amortization period for funding certain past-service costs, and increased employee pension benefits. But instead of disclosing the impact of each of the changes, the company merely stated in its annual report that "while the individual impact of the increase in benefits and the revised actuarial assumptions was significant, the net effect of the changes was not material in relation to the company's net income."

---

[7] The Conference Board, *Financial Management of Company Pension Plans* (New York, 1973).

[8] Patrick J. Regan, "Pension Costs and Unfunded Liabilities—A Special Report," Merrill Lynch, Pierce, Fenner & Smith, Inc., October 2, 1974.

Because of inadequate disclosure, we do not know the extent to which companies used higher interest rate assumptions to hold down pension costs in the late 1960s and the early 1970s. The potential for such easing of the pension expense is, of course, now greatly diminished. The industry norm today for actuarial interest rate assumptions is approximately 5 percent to 6 percent, and this might appear conservative. However, the actuarial assumptions for future wage and salary increases are generally low, on the order of 2 percent to 3 percent a year. Because compensation will probably grow more rapidly than that, the interest rate assumption should be far enough below the market rate of return to provide for greater-than-assumed rates of wage inflation.

In line with the findings of the classic University of Chicago study on rates of return over the 1926–65 period, many executives expect their pension fund equities to garner a 9 percent annual return over the long run.[9] If they can realize such a return, their 5 percent to 6 percent yield assumptions will leave a 3 percent to 4 percent cushion for greater-than-expected rates of inflation. Unfortunately, 9 percent market rates of return have not been very common in recent years. For example, an A. G. Becker study of the performance of some 3,000 institutional investors showed that their average annual return was nil for the ten-year period that ended in 1974. Actuarial assumptions are based on historical experience, and the experience of the past decade—spiraling rates of inflation, costly wage settlements, and negligible investment returns—has been disappointing for those who had hoped to offset pension cost increases with increases in yield assumptions.

Keeping in mind the disclosure problems and the noncomparability of the individual company figures, we can now examine the summary statistics on the growth of pension costs.

THE SURVEY OF PENSION COSTS

To determine the size and growth of pension costs and unfunded liabilities for a cross section of American industry, we refer to the Merrill Lynch survey of 40 major corporations.[10] The report ana-

---

[9] Lawrence Fisher and James H. Lorie, "Rates of Return on Investments in Common Stocks: The Year-by-Year Record, 1926–65," *Journal of Business*, vol. 41 (July 1968), pp. 291–316. Reprinted in James Lorie and Richard Brealey, *Modern Developments in Investment Management* (New York: Praeger Publishers, Inc., 1972).

[10] See note 8.

lyzed the pension figures of the four largest companies, ranked by number of employees, in each of ten major industry groups. While it is not claimed that the sample represents the whole population of pension-sponsoring companies, it has the virtue of comprehending a very large part of the total pension assets and liabilities involved and of being representative of companies of greatest investment interest. All but 5 of the 36 industrial and 4 retail companies were among the 100 largest U.S. corporations, and 13 of the 30 Dow Jones Industrial companies were represented. As of the end of 1974, the 40 companies employed nearly 5.4 million people, or one sixth of the labor force affected by ERISA. In addition, the firms had pension assets of over $27 billion, about one fifth of the $134 billion (at cost) held by all private, noninsured pension funds at the end of 1974.[11]

How fast have pension contributions been rising? This was the first matter of concern. As shown in Figure 2–2, the rate of growth in annual pension contributions of the 40 companies accelerated to 19.5 percent in 1974, up sharply from the 12 percent to 15 percent range of the previous three years. The distribution has been shifting to the right, as the growth rates jump four to five percentage points every three years. The three-year comparison is most important because major labor contracts are negotiated every three years. The 1970 contracts translated into a 14 percent increase in 1971 pension costs, and the 1973 contracts produced an increase of 19.5 percent in 1974. Of course, some of the 1974 advance was the result of companies amending their retirement plans to conform to ERISA.

Between 1969 and 1974, four fifths of the companies in the survey experienced at least one year when pension costs rose more than 25 percent. In a typical year about a quarter of the firms sustained such an increase: the sharp advances usually occurred during the first year of a new labor contract. The most recent example was 1974 when no less than 42.5 percent of the 40 companies reported annual pension cost increases of 25 percent or more. The steepest increases occurred at Dow Chemical (where pension costs rose 120 percent), U.S. Steel (up 89 percent), DuPont (up 48 percent), Caterpillar Tractor (up 44 percent), and Honeywell (up 42 percent).

To be sure, there are a few firms each year that experienced

---

[11] See Appendix D for the pension cost and liability figures of the individual companies in the survey.

FIGURE 2–2

Annual growth of pension costs (40 companies, 1969–1974)

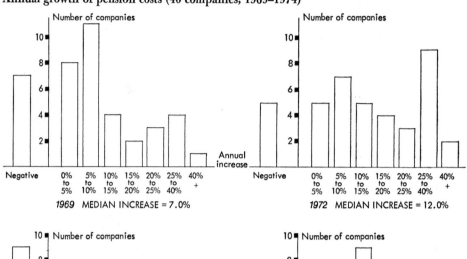

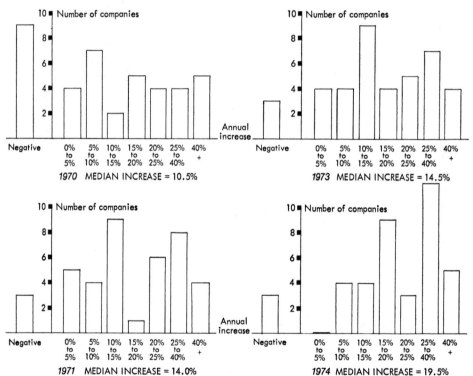

reduced retirement outlays. Sears and J. C. Penney had lower retirement expenditures in 1974, primarily because their retirement plans were built around profit sharing programs with pension plans only supplemental. Although their pension costs rose, their profit sharing contributions declined with pretax profits so that total retirement outlays dropped 9 percent at J. C. Penney and 20 percent at Sears.

On a per-employee basis, the pension contributions varied widely from industry to industry. The typical company in the survey contributed a little over $500 per employee to its retirement plan in 1973, but the contribution jumped 40 percent in 1974 to slightly more than $700. In the industries where new labor contracts went into effect, such as autos and steel, the per-employee contributions rose 20 percent to 25 percent, from a 1973 range of $700 to $1,000 to a 1974 range of $850 to $1,200. On the other hand, retirement contributions in the retail industry, which is characterized by part-time and seasonal employment, were less than $175 per person, on average.

The 1973 and the 1974 retirement contributions, as a percent of pretax profits and on a per-employee basis, are shown in Figure 2–3. In both years, the per-man contributions were heaviest for Bethlehem Steel, Lockheed, Republic Steel, and Western Union. While the average company in the survey reported pension costs equal to 14.5 percent of pretax profits in 1973 and 18 percent in 1974, 4 of the 40 firms had pension expenses equal to more than three quarters of their pretax earnings. In 1974 Chrysler suffered a pretax loss of $136 million after payment of $256 million into the pension fund, Lockheed recorded a pension expense that was nearly three times as large as its pretax profit, and Western Union and Uniroyal had annual pension expenses equal to 98 percent and 78 percent, respectively, of pretax earnings.

The auto industry is an interesting example of what can happen when the profits of a cyclical industry turn down while pension costs rise sharply in the first year of a new labor contract. In 1974, pension expense as a percent of pretax profits rose from 16 percent to 49 percent at General Motors, from 21 percent to 66 percent at Ford, from 28 percent to 59 percent at American Motors, and from 44 percent to the deficit situation at Chrysler.

Because pretax profits are net of pension costs, it is sometimes helpful to examine pension expense as a percentage of the two

FIGURE 2–3

Pension contributions as a percent of pretax profits and per employee

	Pension contribution			
	As a percent of pretax profits		*Per employee*	
	1974	*1973*	*1974*	*1973*
General Motors......................	49%	16%	$1,115	$ 887
Ford..............................	66	21	829	708
Chrysler...........................	Deficit	44	1,002	736
American Motors....................	59	28	747	740
DuPont............................	22	10	1,097	855
Union Carbide......................	10	12	796	586
Monsanto..........................	8	9	775	616
Dow...............................	6	6	1,227	596
Warner Lambert.....................	9	8	411	348
Johnson & Johnson..................	6	5	289	271
American Home Products.............	3	4	297	367
Pfizer.............................	7	6	397	313
General Electric....................	17	13	415	349
Westinghouse......................	36	21	377	472
Combustion Engineering.............	23	18	409	396
Babcock & Wilcox..................	45	62	655	603
Beatrice Foods.....................	8	8	312	269
Kraftco...........................	13	10	454	402
General Foods......................	11	8	545	401
Borden...........................	8	8	285	237
Caterpillar Tractor..................	24	16	1,151	829
Eastman Kodak.....................	24	9	2,187	2,067
Lockheed..........................	287	403	1,610	1,181
Western Union.....................	98	69	2,154	1,971
IBM..............................	10	9	1,142	941
Sperry Rand.......................	23	22	589	472
Honeywell.........................	34	15	450	299
Xerox.............................	13	14	961	980
Sears.............................	18	16	326	353
Penney............................	14	10	155	165
Kresge............................	6	3	86	70
Woolworth.........................	14	10	137	122
U.S. Steel.........................	16	18	907	487
Bethlehem Steel....................	25	32	1,261	979
Armco Steel.......................	15	25	1,052	889
Republic Steel.....................	18	34	1,243	1,162
Goodyear..........................	26	17	514	388
Firestone..........................	19	14	425	342
Uniroyal...........................	78	74	1,006	829
Goodrich..........................	44	33	810	693

added together, or "funds available for pension costs." When pension costs are equal to one third or 33 percent of "funds available," approximately one dollar is contributed to the pension fund and one dollar is paid in federal income taxes for every dollar that is reported as earnings. Seven of the 40 companies in the survey were over the 33 percent mark in 1974, including the 4 automobile manufacturers, as well as Lockheed, Western Union, and Uniroyal. The median figure for the 40 companies in 1973 was 12.5 percent, indicating that for every eight dollars of "funds available," one dollar

FIGURE 2–4

Pension contributions as a percent of funds available and as a percent of pretax profits (40 companies, 1974)

Range	Pension contributions as a percent of funds available		Pension contributions as a percent of pretax profits	
	No. of firms	*Percent of firms*	*No. of firms*	*Percent of firms*
0% to 5%.................	1	2.5	1	2.5
5% to 10%.................	10	25.0	8	20.0
10% to 15%.................	8	20.0	7	17.5
15% to 20%.................	7	17.5	6	15.0
20% to 25%.................	3	7.5	5	12.5
25% to 40%.................	6	15.0	4	10.0
40% and over...............	5	12.5	9	22.5
	40	100.0	40	100.0
Median.....................	15.5%		18.0%	

was placed in the pension fund and seven dollars were reported as pretax income. As shown in Figure 2–4, the typical pension fund garnered more than one out of every seven dollars available in 1974, instead of one out of eight, as in 1973.

In December 1974, the Financial Accounting Standards Board ruled that companies had to disclose in their annual reports whether or not they expected ERISA to have a material impact on their pension costs. We examined several hundred annual reports and found that very few large corporations expected a material increase in pension costs due to ERISA, and for those few the expected increases were confined pretty much to the 10 percent to 15 percent range. For example, the Gannett Company estimated that ERISA would add 10 percent to its annual pension bill; Westinghouse foresaw a 10 percent to 15 percent jump; and Abbott Laboratories, R. J. Reynolds, and Texas Instruments looked for an increase of approximately 15 percent. Of the companies we examined, the only ones that expected pension costs to rise by more than 15 percent were in the retailing industry. F. W. Woolworth expected an 18 percent increase in pension costs over the figure for the year ended January 31, 1975, while J. C. Penney prepared for a 27 percent advance and S. S. Kresge predicted a 32 percent increase. Because of its unique characteristics, with high turnover rates and considerable part-time and seasonal employment, the retail industry was greatly affected by ERISA's more stringent eligibility and vesting standards. But even with the large percentage increases, the pension costs of retail companies will still be among the lowest in terms of contributions per employee.

We examined only major corporations, and it appears that ERISA will have a greater impact on the smaller firms. For example, the *Institutional Investor* magazine conducted a survey of pension funds in December 1974 and found that the administrators of the large pension funds (i.e., those with more than $300 million in assets) expected their total pension costs to rise as a result of ERISA less than 4 percent, whereas at the smaller funds, the expected increase was in the 5 percent to 6 percent range.[12]

While large and rapidly growing, the required contributions are still manageable for most large companies. However, as we shall show, the numbers presented so far are not a meaningful measure of the real pension burden.

---

[12] "How Hard Will the New Pension Law Pinch?" *Institutional Investor*, December 1974, p. 23. In a more recent survey 44 percent of the funds over the $100 million mark indicated that their pension costs rose less than 2 percent because of ERISA, whereas only a third of the smaller funds held the increase to 2 percent. However, more than three-quarters of all the funds experienced an increase of less than 5 percent. See "The Costs of ERISA," *Institutional Investor*, February 1976, p. 47.

Chapter 3

Unfunded liabilities—
A financial time-bomb

Although rising pension contributions have remained a major concern, unfunded liabilities command even greater attention in the wake of the passage of ERISA. The principal change wrought by the act was the transformation of the financial status of unfunded pension liabilities from gratuities into corporate obligations. In effect, ERISA added a new element of leverage into the capital structures of the plan-sponsoring companies. In this chapter, we consider the disclosure and measurement problems associated with unfunded pension liabilities, examine the published figures of the 40 sample companies, and adjust the capital structures of the firms to reflect the leverage introduced by ERISA.

DISCLOSURE AND MEASUREMENT PROBLEMS

The size of a company's unfunded pension liability depends, among other things, on how it values the pension assets and how it computes the total liability. In the first two chapters, we noted that the present value of the liability can be altered by changing the funding method or the actuarial assumptions. Thus, when companies raised their interest rate assumptions en masse in the late 1960s and early 1970s, the effect was to reduce both their annual pension costs and their unfunded liabilities.

On the asset side, there are numerous actuarial methods for valuing the pension fund assets. According to the Conference Board's

1973 study of pension funds, 46 percent of the 117 plan-sponsoring companies valued their pension assets at cost, 22 percent used market value, 18 percent followed a long-range appreciation method, and 14 percent used other methods.[1]

The difference between the market value and the book value of the assets of the typical pension fund can be substantial. The Securities and Exchange Commission conducts an annual survey of all private, noninsured pension funds and publishes the aggregate asset valuation figures.[2] According to the survey, such pension funds had $36.8 billion of unrealized appreciation at the end of 1972, as the market value of their holdings was $154.3 billion and the cost was only $117.5 billion. Total unrealized gains slipped to $5.7 billion in 1973 and turned into a $22 billion unrealized loss in 1974, when the market value of the assets, at $111.7 billion, was nearly 17 percent below the $133.7 billion cost.

From World War II until 1974, pension funds had never had an aggregate unrealized loss. Thus it was generally considered conservative policy to value the assets at cost or cost adjusted for a "programmed" amount of annual appreciation, such as 5 percent or 6 percent. General Electric uses the latter approach and carries its pension assets at "amortized cost plus programmed appreciation in the common stock portfolio, the recognition of which is limited by a maximum ratio, calculated on a moving basis, of book to market values over a multiyear period."[3] For example, in 1973, GE programmed or recognized common stock appreciation of $68.6 million, of which $34.2 represented realized gains and $34.4 million represented accrued gains. In 1974, it programmed $79.2 million in appreciation, comprised of $7 million in realized losses and $86.2 million in accrued gains. At the end of 1974, the "adjusted" carrying cost of the pension fund was nearly $2.8 billion. Subtracting the assets from the total vested benefits of approximately $3.1 billion, GE reported that its 1974 liability for unfunded vested benefits was only $345 million. But the market value of the pension fund was $415 million below the adjusted book value at the end of 1974, indicating that the liability for unfunded vested benefits would have

---

[1] The Conference Board, *Financial Management of Company Pension Plans* (New York, 1973).

[2] The survey appears in the April issue of the *SEC Statistical Bulletin,* a publication of the Securities and Exchange Commission.

[3] General Electric 1974 Annual Report, p. 34.

been twice as great, $760 million, if the assets had been valued at market. Similarly, U.S. Steel listed a 1974 unfunded vested liability of $400 million, based on vested benefits of approximately $4 billion and pension assets of $3.6 billion. But the $3.6 billion figure was calculated as a 12-quarter average of the market value of quoted securities, and at cost or less for other assets. At the end of 1974, the market value of the fund was approximately $2.8 billion, and on that basis the unfunded vested liability would have been $1.2 billion instead of the reported $400 million.

Our purpose in discussing these variations is to show that reported pension liability figures for different companies are often not comparable and not to imply that General Electric or U.S. Steel use improper or unusual actuarial valuation methods. Prior to the 1973–74 bear market in stock prices, such smoothing devices produced asset valuations that were generally more conservative than market valuations. But market value is more important under ERISA, and cost valuations or smoothing techniques can result in understated liability figures in a bear market. For valuations in a bull market, the opposite is of course true.

The 1973–74 bear market produced some statistical anomalies for the many firms that value pension assets on a market basis when computing unfunded vested benefits, but use an actuarial cost basis when computing unfunded past-service costs. The unfunded past-service costs include benefits that are already vested and benefits that are expected to become vested. Hence the liability for unfunded past-service costs (UPSC) will always exceed the unfunded vested benefits (UVB) figure when the pension assets are valued on the same basis in both computations. However, in a bear market, the UVB can exceed the UPSC if the pension assets are valued at market in the UVB calculation, but at cost in the UPSC computation (assuming the market value of the assets is considerably below cost). This actually happened to the Sears' supplemental pension plan in 1974. The UVB, on a market valuation basis, was $115 million, while the UPSC, on an actuarial cost basis, was only $48.7 million.

The UPSC figure is of interest primarily because it is amortized and charged against income annually. For example, B. F. Goodrich had a $321 million UPSC at the end of 1974, which it was amortizing over a 30-year period. Hence over a quarter of its $40 million pension expense represented the amortization of the UPSC.

The UPSC can be reduced by portfolio appreciation, but the liability tends to increase sharply every few years, as new labor contracts are signed and employees are given additional pension benefits for years of past service. For example, if a new contract calls for an increase in pension benefits from $10 to $12 a month for every year of service, the total pension liability would rise 20 percent, other things being equal. Suppose that prior to the contract, the total pension liability was estimated at $100 million and the pension fund was valued at $80 million, for a UPSC of $20 million. If the liability were increased by 20 percent to $120 million and the value of the pension assets remained unchanged, the UPSC would double, from $20 to $40 million. By way of example, General Motors signed a pact with the United Auto Workers in 1973 that called for higher pension benefits and contained the "30 years service and out" provision covering early retirement with full benefits. As a result, General Motors' UPSC rose from $3 billion at the end of 1972 to $4.1 billion in 1973 and $6.1 billion at year-end 1974.

Sears, Goodrich, and General Motors are often noted for outstanding disclosure in their annual reports to shareholders. Although they disclose their unfunded past-service costs, many firms do not, for *Accounting Principles Board Opinion No. 8* only requires the disclosure of unfunded vested benefits. Because the UPSC does not have to be disclosed, firms with large unfunded liabilities and weak vesting provisions often appear to be fully funded, as they simply report that pension assets exceed vested benefits.

THE SURVEY OF PENSION LIABILITIES

Of the 40 companies in the Merrill Lynch survey, 33 revealed their unfunded past-service costs in their 1974 annual or 10-K reports. Table 3–1 shows that the average firm had a UPSC equal to 19 percent of its net worth in 1974, as compared to the 15 percent of 1973. The table also indicates that the typical company had an unfunded vested liability equal to 5 percent of net worth at the end of 1974, up from zero in 1973.

At the end of 1973, half of the 40 companies in the survey were fully funded as regards vested benefits, whereas at the end of 1974 only a quarter of the companies were fully funded. Among the industries for which vested benefits were substantially funded at the end of 1973, the chemical, food processing, office equipment, and retail groups became modestly underfunded in 1974, as the bear

TABLE 3–1

Unfunded vested benefits and unfunded past-service costs as a percent of net worth (sample of 40 large companies, based on 1974 and fiscal 1975 figures)

	Unfunded vested benefits as a percent of net worth		Unfunded past-service costs as a percent of net worth	
Range	*No. of firms*	*Percent of firms*	*No. of firms*	*Percent of firms*
Not available...............	1	2.5	7	17.5
None......................	10	25.0	2	5.0
0% to 5%.................	9	22.5	6	15.0
5% to 10%................	5	12.5	3	7.5
10% to 20%...............	2	5.0	7	17.5
20% to 30%...............	7	17.5	2	5.0
30% to 50%...............	4	10.0	8	20.0
50% and over..............	2	5.0	5	12.5
	40	100.0	40	100.0
Median unfunded liability as a percent of net worth..............	5%		19%	

market trimmed the value of pension assets. The only industry in the survey in which all four companies were fully funded as to vested benefits at the end of both 1973 and 1974 was the drug group.

As shown in Table 3–1, the average company in the survey had a liability for unfunded vested benefits (UVB) equal to 5 percent of net worth. But 6 of the 40 companies had UVB's that exceeded the critical 30 percent of net worth figure. The 6 were Lockheed (where the UVB was 16 times as great as stockholder's equity), Uniroyal (UVB equal to 78 percent of net worth), Chrysler (45 percent), Bethlehem Steel (41 percent), Western Union (40 percent), and Republic Steel (34 percent.)

The unfunded liabilities should also be considered in relation to the size of the pension fund. At the end of 1974, the 40 companies in the survey held over $27 billion in pension assets but had an aggregate UVB of approximately $12 billion and an aggregate UPSC of some $20 billion.[4] The $12 billion UVB was equal to 44 percent of the $27.4 billion in pension assets, most of which were valued at

---

[4] Most companies did not disclose the value of their pension assets in their annual and 10-K reports. Thus, the $27.4 billion figure for total pension assets was based partially on figures published on individual companies in the Money Market Directory. Some of the asset figures were at cost and some were at market. See Appendix D for details on individual companies.

cost and did not reflect the market losses of 1973–74. Hence the figures suggest that the pension fund of the typical company in the survey would have had to advance perhaps 50 percent from year-end 1974 levels to cover the 1974 level of vested benefits. The popular stock market indices rose 32 percent to 38 percent, in 1975, but according to SEC figures, the typical fund had only 56 percent of its assets in equities at end of 1974 and so did not get the full benefit of the stock market advance.[5]

The pension asset figures change daily with the fluctuations of the stock and bond markets, and the vested benefits tend to rise with each new labor contract. To understand the real trend in unfunded vested liabilities, creditors, analysts, and investors should examine the market value of the pension fund and the present value of the vested benefits. Unfortunately, *Accounting Principles Board Opinion No. 8* requires only the disclosure of the net difference between the two figures, the liability for unfunded vested benefits. Among the 40 companies surveyed, only 15 firms revealed in their annual and 10-K reports the value of their pension assets, and in most cases it was book rather than market value. However, by adding the market value of the pension assets to the UVB (computed on a market basis) we were able to estimate the present value of total vested benefits for the seven companies in Table 3–2. The table shows the 1974 year-end market value of each company's pension fund, the estimate of total vested benefits, and the amount the fund would have had to appreciate to fully fund the 1974 level of vested benefits. For example, a 14 percent increase in the year-end market value of Eastman Kodak's pension fund would have covered the 1974 vested benefits of $1.085 billion. By contrast, Bethlehem Steel's $604 million pension fund would have had to nearly triple to cover its $1.633 billion in vested benefits. Vested benefits exceeded the market value of pension assets by $760 million at General Electric and by $648 million at Westinghouse. However, GE was in a much better position because its pension fund was three and a half times as large as that of Westinghouse and needed only 32 percent appreciation to cover the 1974 level of vested benefits, whereas Westinghouse needed a 96 percent advance.

Lockheed's situation is especially interesting. At the end of 1974, Lockheed had a pension fund with a market value of $625 million,

---

[5] Securities and Exchange Commission, "Private Noninsured Pension Funds, 1974," *SEC Statistical Bulletin*, April 1975.

TABLE 3–2

Amount of asset appreciation required to fully fund vested benefits (1974 data)

Company	Market value of pension fund (millions)	Estimated vested benefits (millions)	Appreciation required to fund VB's
Eastman Kodak	$ 955	$1,085	14%
General Electric	2,347	3,107	32
U.S. Steel	2,800	4,000	43
Lockheed	625	1,045	67
Westinghouse	673	1,321	96
Republic Steel	347	769	122
Bethlehem Steel	604	1,633	170

Source: 1974 annual and 10-K reports.

a UVB of $420 million, and a corporate net worth of a mere $26.5 million. In the first quarter of 1975, though, the portfolio appreciated $85 million and the UVB was reduced by a like amount, from $420 million to $335 million. An analyst who merely compared Lockheed's $420 million UVB to its $26.5 million net worth might have considered the situation bleak. However, the pension fund was large enough that a 50 percent advance in a bull market could have substantially solved the problem.

THE ADJUSTED CAPITAL STRUCTURE

Because ERISA creates a potentially senior claim on corporate as well as pension assets, it is necessary to adjust the capital structures of plan-sponsoring companies to reflect unfunded guaranteed benefits. In the event that a pension plan is terminated, the Pension Benefit Guaranty Corporation (PBGC) stands ready to make good any unfunded guaranteed benefits. Under the current provisions of ERISA, the PBGC can then attach a lien on the corporate assets of the plan-sponsoring company, limited to the lesser of the unfunded guaranteed benefits or 30 percent of the company's net assets.

Precise figures on unfunded guaranteed benefits are not available, but we can use unfunded vested benefits as a proxy. Because the PBGC has a five-year phase-in rule for benefits that result from plan amendments, a $750 per month maximum benefit per plan participant, and several other limiting provisions, unfunded guaranteed benefits could be less than unfunded vested benefits in a termination. On the other hand, unfunded guaranteed benefits could exceed unfunded vested benefits if valuation of the latter took place when stock and bond prices were considerably higher than on the termination date.

Despite these difficulties and the fact that different companies use different funding methods, actuarial assumptions, eligibility standards, and vesting provisions, we gathered published figures for the 40-company sample and adjusted the firms' capital structures to reflect their unfunded vested pension benefits.[6] The figures, which are shown in Table 3–3, are based on year-end 1974 or fiscal 1975 data. In each case, we included in the capital structure the liability for unfunded vested benefits and reduced stockholder's equity by a like amount, subject to the 30 percent of net worth limitation. Hence, the "adjusted" capital structure was equal to the liability for unfunded vested benefits (UVB), the long-term debt (LTD), and the "adjusted" stockholders' equity (SE). As shown in the table, the typical firm in the survey had a long-term capital structure of 23 percent long-term debt and 77 percent equity before the adjustment. After the adjustment, the typical capital structure was composed of 9 percent unfunded vested pension liability, 23 percent long-term debt, and 68 percent "adjusted" stockholders' equity. In effect, the typical firm with $100 in long-term capital had $23 in long-term debt and $77 in equity. It had a UVB equal to $9, which, when subtracted from the $77 in equity, left an "adjusted" equity of $68. The long-term debt remained fixed at $23. In most cases, the UVB was a minor portion of the adjusted capital structure; but for nearly a quarter of the firms, it accounted for 16 percent to 25 percent of the adjusted capital structure, placing debt holders in a potentially subordinate position.

The table shows the 40 companies ranked on the basis of their adjusted debt-to-equity ratios, with the combined UVB and long-term debt in relation to the adjusted stockholders' equity. We ranked the companies in order to provide a distribution of the adjusted debt-to-equity ratios. However, we must reiterate our earlier caveat regarding the difference in the methods used by the companies in computing their unfunded vested benefits.

With the problem of noncomparability in mind, we concentrated on the median figures. After the UVB adjustments, the typical firm

---

[6] Table 3 appeared in Patrick J. Regan, "Potential Corporate Liabilities under ERISA," *Financial Analysts Journal,* March–April 1976.

TABLE 3–3

Capital structure and debt-to-equity ratios, after adjustment for unfunded vested pension liabilities (40 company sample, 1974 data)

	Debt-to-equity ratio		Adjusted capital structure		
Company	*Before UVB*	*After UVB*	*UVB*	*LTD*	*SE*
Lockheed.....................	31.38	45.39*	1%	97%	2%
Western Union................	1.16	2.09*	14	54	32
Uniroyal.....................	.77	1.53*	17	44	39
Babcock & Wilcox.............	.73	1.44	17	42	41
B. F. Goodrich...............	.66	1.13	13	40	47
Chrysler.....................	.37	.96*	22	27	51
Caterpillar Tractor...........	.45	.90	17	31	52
Goodyear.....................	.53	.89	12	35	53
Westinghouse.................	.44	.87	16	30	54
Dow Chemical.................	.66	.81	5	40	55
Bethlehem Steel...............	.26	.80*	24	21	55
Republic Steel................	.22	.74*	25	18	58
Ford.........................	.24	.62	19	19	62
Xerox........................	.59	.59	0	37	63
Firestone.....................	.44	.56	6	30	64
American Motors..............	.21	.52	17	17	66
F. W. Woolworth..............	.44	.52	4	30	66
Honeywell....................	.46	.52	2	32	66
Borden.......................	.42	.48	3	29	68
General Motors...............	.07	.47	25	7	68
General Electric...............	.32	.46	7	24	69
Armco Steel..................	.24	.45	11	20	69
U.S. Steel....................	.30	.43	7	23	70
Sperry Rand..................	.43	.43	0	30	70
Monsanto.....................	.33	.39	3	25	72
Union Carbide................	.36	.39	2	26	72
Beatrice Foods................	.32	.33	1	24	75
Kraftco......................	.28	.31	2	22	76
Combustion Engineering........	.30	n.a.	n.a.	23	77
Pfizer.......................	.30	.30	0	23	77
General Foods................	.29	.29	0	22	78
J. C. Penny..................	.26	.26	0	21	79
Sears........................	.21	.24	2	17	81
Kresge.......................	.21	.21	0	17	83
DuPont.......................	.21	.21	0	17	83
Warner Lambert...............	.11	.11	0	10	90
Eastman Kodak................	.03	.07	4	3	93
IBM.........................	.03	.05	2	3	95
Johnson & Johnson............	.04	.04	0	3	97
American Home Products........	No LTD or UVB		0	0	100
Average......................	.30	.47	9	23	68

UVB—unfunded vested pension liability.
LTD—long-term debt.
SE—adjusted stockholders' equity, or stockholders' equity minus UVB.
n.a.—not available.
* UVB is limited to 30 percent of net worth.

in the survey had a debt-to-equity ratio of 0.47, a jump of more than 50 percent from the preadjustment ratio of 0.30. Furthermore, in 7 of the 40 cases, the debt-to-equity ratio more than doubled, and in 4 other instances it nearly doubled. The sharpest increases took place in the auto industry and to a lesser extent, in the steel, the tire and rubber, and the electrical equipment groups. As shown in the table, these were the groups that, by and large, had the highest debt-to-equity ratios prior to the adjustment. The drug and the retail groups had the lowest debt-to-equity ratios, both before and after the adjustments.[7]

According to the Federal Trade Commission's *Quarterly Financial Report,* the debt-to-equity ratio of the average manufacturing corporation jumped more than 50 percent between 1965 and 1970, from 0.28 to 0.44, and then stabilized for five years. If our sample companies are representative and the typical debt-to-equity ratio rises more than 50 percent when the unfunded vested pension liability is incorporated into the capital structure, then we can conclude that corporate balance sheets suffered as much potential damage with the passage of ERISA as they had in the previous ten years. For corporate executives, bankers, security, and credit analysts and investors, this is a major impact of ERISA.

---

[7] Federal Trade Commission, *Quarterly Financial Report* (quarterly issues, 1965 to 1975).

Part 2

Blueprint for a sound structure

Chapter 4

A descriptive financial framework of pension claims
(or why pre-ERISA some pension claims were unlikely to be paid)

"The book value of a common stock was originally the most important element in its financial exhibit. It was supposed to show 'the value' of the shares in the same way as a merchant's balance sheet shows him the value of his business. This idea has almost completely disappeared from the financial horizon. The value of a company's assets as carried in its balance sheet has lost practically all its significance. This change arose from the fact, first, that the value of the fixed assets, as stated, frequently bore no relationship to the actual cost and, second, that in an even larger proportion of cases these values bore no relationship to the figure at which they could be sold or the figure which would be justified by the earnings."[1]

It is clear from Part 1 that the potential burden of the pension plan is important. But *how* important and *who* bears the burden? That depends on how pension claims are treated. We are fully aware that before ERISA a pension beneficiary's legal claim was against the pension fund and not the assets of the employer corporation. Yet, in practice, the system generally functioned as if the claim did extend to corporate assets. The beneficiary expected sufficient employer contributions to fund his or her claim, and society expected the company to pay such claims as they fell due.

---

[1] Benjamin Graham and David L. Dodd, *Security Analysis* (New York: McGraw-Hill Book Co., 1940), pp. 573–74.

On the other hand, the pension beneficiary's claim was not a conventional lender's claim against the corporation. Until ERISA, it was virtually ignored by corporate lenders and security analysts (as we shall see, for good reason). With ERISA they can no longer afford to do so. But to understand why, we must first understand the nature of a lender's claim against a corporation:

1. Because a lender's entire principal, as well as current interest, is at risk, a lender cannot safely confine himself to looking at current flows (e.g., comparing the annual interest expense or the debt service to earnings before interest and taxes have). The basic question of security for a lender is one of stocks rather than flows.

2. The lender must ask himself or herself: How does the value of the lender's claim compare with what the underlying security could be sold for in foreclosure? If we assume that markets are reasonably efficient, then current market prices will be useful guides in answering this question.

3. This is true even when the loan in question is secured by the general credit of the borrower, in which case it is the value of the borrowing corporation itself to which the lender must look for protection. If the lender's claim is junior to other claims on the general credit, then it is the value of the corporation *less* the value of the senior claims to which the lender must look.

4. The market value of a corporation fluctuates from day to day. This does not diminish the relevance of current market value for the lender, because this value impounds everything known about the borrower, including all past market values. This does raise the possibility, however, that *future* market values will be less than the current market value—a possibility that constitutes the fundamental risk for a lender.

5. In bankruptcy, a borrower will sometimes be worth more as a going concern, sometimes more with his or her assets liquidated piecemeal. It may or may not be true that market value reflects the worth of the firm on a going concern rather than a piecemeal basis, but the value relevant to creditors (i.e., the greater of these two values) will never be *less* than the market value.

6. Whether the security in question is an entire firm or a specific asset, accounting book value will rarely, if ever, be superior to current market value as an estimate of what a lender could sell his or her security for, if he or she were to foreclose today.

How much his or her claim is really worth (as opposed to its cost or its face value) is of critical importance to the lender. But what is the relevance of this question for the executive of the borrowing corporation? For the security analyst estimating the value of the corporation's shares?

In arm's-length dealing, a rational lender will be unwilling to accommodate a borrower unless the value of the claim created by the loan exceeds the amount of the loan. But the corporation's ability to borrow is measured by the lender's willingness to lend. The value of the equity in the corporation is the residual remaining after existing lenders' claims have been subtracted from the gross economic value of the corporation. Hence, we can draw two conclusions from our discussion of lending principles:

1. Any change in the value of the lenders' claims affects the value of the residual equity, and thus the value of the corporation's shares.

2. The value of the residual equity remaining after *existing* lenders' claims measures what the corporation can give *future* lenders in return for still further loans to the corporation. Thus the residual equity at market value is an upper limit on the corporation's as yet untapped borrowing power—a number of more than token interest to corporate executives. Since this number fluctuates unpredictably from day to day, the corporation's future borrowing power is to this extent also unpredictable.

VALUATION OF ASSETS

It follows from these considerations that although there are several ways to view the worth of any asset, there is only one pertinent way—market value. In other words, an asset is worth only what a willing buyer will pay for it. Market value reflects the present discounted worth of the economic benefits.

Book value is irrelevant, for it is an accountant's concept based on an entirely different premise, that of historical cost. The accountant's principal concern is the amortization of cost over the useful life of the asset, which rarely relates to economic reality.

As pointed out in the previous section, the lender is concerned with the market value of the underlying asset, not its original cost (as anyone who has ever attempted to obtain a loan can attest).

When a company invests a dollar in plant, for example, does it base the capital budgeting decision on historical or expected income from the investment? Is the risk element used to discount the return stream based on history or current expectations? Just as these decisions are based on current and future expectations, so it is with the purchase of any asset for economic use.

Because of the unpredictable character of market value fluctuations, today's value is the best basis for an estimate of tomorrow's value, and so on. It is the relevant number even though it depends in part on economic and market forces wholly external to the assets being valued. We live in a dynamic world shaped by such unpredictable influences as wars, famines, changing monetary and fiscal policies, and changes in technology and consumer tastes. A static valuation method ignores this reality. Other things equal, a security purchased in a 4 percent interest rate environment will be worth less in an 8 percent environment, and a security issued when the company's prospects were bright will be worth less when prospects dim. In short, changes in expectations produce changes in market values.

In a period of rising interest rates companies often take advantage of differences between book and market values and reduce debt outstanding by purchasing in the open market their own bonds selling at deep discounts. In 1973 and 1974, companies such as General Host, United Brands, and Western Union engineered debenture swaps that required minimal cash outlay but cleared the books of millions of dollars of debt. In June 1973, Western Union offered holders of its 5¼ percent debentures $100 cash and $560 principal amount of a new 10¾ percent debenture for each $1,000 principal amount of the 5¼ percent debentures. Because the market value of the latter was only $570 at the time of the offering, eager bondholders swapped $62 million of the old bonds for $6 million in cash and $35 million of the new bonds. In effect, Western Union wrote down some of its outstanding debt from book to market value, and thereby reduced its debt load by $21 million.

The accountant is not the only professional involved in the book value versus market value controversy. When valuing pension claims and assets—and particularly in making the actuarial interest assumption—the actuaries tend to ignore market prices. Because actuaries assume a correlation between past returns and future returns, they apply "smoothing techniques" to the valuation of pension portfolios and base their assumptions about future portfolio returns on past history. Yet, almost all studies of financial markets indicate that there is no correlation between historical returns and future returns and that asset prices tend to fluctuate unpredictably.[2]

THE PENSION BURDEN PRIOR TO ERISA

Since corporate pension assets are commonly invested at least in part in risky assets (i.e., common stocks), are the beneficiaries automatically in jeopardy?

Consider the analogy between pension beneficiaries and bank deposits. Loan defaults occur, and the rate of default is sensitive to economic and market conditions overall, so that even a highly diversified loan portfolio is risky.

Yet in a properly run bank, depositors' claims can truly be said to be virtually riskless—even in the absence of a Federal Deposit Insurance Corporation. The reason is that a well-run bank maintains equity capital sufficiently large in relation to its deposits to absorb any losses incurred in the loan portfolio.

In similar fashion, the corporation can encourage risk taking in its pension portfolio without jeopardizing the beneficiaries so long as:

1. Pension beneficiaries are considered to have a claim on the general credit of the corporation in the event that assets in the pension portfolio prove inadequate.
2. The going-concern value of the corporation is adequate to meet the pension and other claims.

Whether the second condition is satisfied is most easily determined in terms of what we may call the *augmented corporate*

---

[2] In an efficient market where information is freely available, the market price of a security can be expected to approximate its "intrinsic" value because of competition among investors. Intrinsic values can change as a result of new information. If, however, there is only gradual propagation of new information and awareness of its implications, past asset price changes will be correlated with future ones. If the adjustment to information is virtually instantaneous, successive price changes will be random.

Random does not mean uncaused nor does it mean that returns on average will be zero. Historically, returns have been randomly distributed around a nonzero mean—something akin to a coin so constructed that on average heads come up six times in ten but with the probability of a head on any toss totally unaffected by the outcome of previous tosses. We are not concerned with the average magnitude of price changes, only their sequence.

For further discussion, see the following: James Lorie and Mary Hamilton, *The Stock Market—Theories and Evidence* (Homewood, Ill.: Richard D. Irwin, Inc., 1973); and Richard A. Brealey, *An Introduction to Risk and Return from Common Stocks* (MIT Press, 1969; 3d printing, 1972).

balance sheet (see Figure 4–1)[3] which includes pension and corporate assets, and pension and corporate liabilities. On the left-hand side of the balance sheet we have the assets of the corporation—measured, however, at market rather than book value and augmented by the current market value of the pension portfolio. On the right-hand side of the balance sheet we have the usual claims of corporate creditors, but augmented by the present value of the pension obligations. In the augmented balance sheet the residual equity available to corporate shareholders is the margin of protection for the pension beneficiaries. (The introduction of the pen-

FIGURE 4–1

Augmented balance sheet (all assets at current market value)

Assets	*Liabilities*
Pension portfolio	Present value of pension obligations
Corporate assets	Corporate liabilities
	Corporate equity* (plugged figure)

* Because equity is a residual, it will generally be different for the augmented and original corporate balance sheets.

sion assets on the left side and the present value of pension claims on the right will generally change the residual equity.)

The key to interpreting the augmented balance sheet is the present value of the pension claims. The rate at which future obligations are discounted back to the present is critical. The appropriate discount rate is the riskless interest rate. If one considers that the corporation has no obligation to protect pension beneficiaries against inflation, then the appropriate discount rate is the rate on government obligations of comparable maturity. If, on the other hand, one considers that the current statement of future pension obligations is really a statement expressed in current dollars of future obligations the real value of which is understood to be fixed, then the appropriate discount rate is the riskless interest rate with inflationary expectations removed—a rate commonly estimated at roughly 3 percent. A more common way to take inflationary ex-

---

[3] The augmented balance sheet concept was first introduced in Walter Bagehot, "Risk in Corporate Pension Funds," *Financial Analysts Journal*, January–February 1972. Walter Bagehot is the pseudonym of one of the authors of this book.

pectations into account is to adjust both the wage and asset return assumptions. It is critical, however, that the gap between the wage and return assumptions not exceed 3 percentage points, for the reason cited previously. Thus, a company that uses a 6 percent interest rate assumption should apply at least a 3 percent wage assumption, so as to maintain the 3 percent spread.[4]

The present value that results from discounting at the appropriate rate is an estimate of the market value of the assets on which the beneficiaries must have a claim if they are not to be subjected to investment risk. If the assets available exceed the present value of future pension claims only when the latter are discounted at a higher rate, the expected proceeds from the assets will fail to meet the claims unless the assets are invested aggressively, with the attendant possibility of loss. Because the riskless rate represents the highest return one can be certain of getting, it enables us to calculate the magnitude of current pension assets necessary to *guarantee* that future obligations can be met.

Under defined benefit pension plans, the corporation guarantees not its contributions but the payment of the future obligations. The only way this guarantee can be meaningful is if the assets available to meet these obligations exceed this magnitude *at every point in time.* Any corporation that is insolvent in the sense of the augmented corporate balance sheet is imposing risks on the beneficiaries for which they are unlikely to get fully rewarded.

Unlike conventional corporate creditors, pension beneficiaries are not in a position to force reorganization of the corporation whenever the margin is threatened by suspending their willingness to lend. Because of this, pension beneficiaries have been virtually powerless to prevent employers from sliding into insolvency in this sense—even though in some cases it ultimately prevented them from collecting their pension benefits.

---

[4] Some companies argue that the riskless rate for them is the rate guaranteed by major insurance companies. Indeed, several firms noted in their 1974 annual reports that their unfunded vested pension liabilities would have been much smaller if they had liquidated the pension assets and used the proceeds to purchase contracts from insurance companies. The latter were able to guarantee annual rates of 8 percent to 9 percent only because bond yields were in the 9 percent to 10 percent range, implying expected rates of inflation of 6 percent to 7 percent. To be sure, if a plan terminates, the dollar value of pension claims is frozen, and no adjustment in the nominal value of the claim for depreciation in the value of the dollar subsequent to termination is required. If, on the other hand, the plan does not terminate, it is usually the real, rather than the nominal, value of the claim that must be paid. Thus, the insurance contract is more likely to cover the ultimate value of the claim if termination occurs soon enough to prevent the nominal value of the claim from reflecting the full impact of inflation.

FIGURE 4–2

ABC CORPORATION
Augmented Balance Sheet
December 31, 1975
(all figures in millions of dollars)

Assets		*Liabilities and Stockholders' Equities*	
Current assets..............	$ 694.1	Current liabilities............	$ 359.5
		Long-term debt..............	630.3
Fixed assets................	1,601.7	Stockholders' equity*.........	1,306.0
Total Assets...........	$2,295.8	Total Liabilities and Stockholders' Equity...	$2,295.8

* Twenty-three million common shares outstanding.

Let us consider the application of the augmented balance sheet to a real though slightly disguised example. In Figure 4–2 we have the conventional corporate balance sheet of firm ABC, with all figures at book value. The market value balance sheet, shown in Figure 4–3, is the second step. By adding stockholders' equity ($717.8 million) and long-term debt ($592 million), both at market value, to current liabilities ($359.5 million), we have the market value of the right-hand side of the balance sheet ($1,699.3 million). Since current assets are essentially valued at market (the inventory question aside), we can subtract the current asset total ($694.1 million) from the sum that appears on the right-hand side of the balance sheet to derive the implied market value of all noncurrent assets (in this case, largely plant and equipment, equal to $975.2 million). These changes are reflected in Figure 4–3.

To that balance sheet we now add the market value of the pension fund as an asset ($421.5 million) and the present value the pension obligations as a liability ($1,070 million). To make the balance sheet balance, we then adjust the market value for the

FIGURE 4–3

ABC CORPORATION
Balance Sheet
December 31, 1975
(all figures in millions of dollars)

Assets		*Liabilities and Stockholders' Equity*	
Current assets..............	$ 694.1	Current liabilities............	$ 359.5
		Long-term debt (m.v.).........	592.0
Fixed assets................	975.2	Stockholders' equity (m.v.)*....	717.8
Total Assets...........	$1,669.3	Total Liabilities and Stockholders' Equity (m.v.)..............	$1,669.3

* Market price of common stock 12/31/75 was $33 per share.

FIGURE 4–4

ABC CORPORATION
Augmented Balance Sheet
December 31, 1975
(all figures in millions of dollars)

Assets		*Liability and Stockholders' Equity*	
Pension fund assets............	$ 421.5	Present value of vested	
Current assets................	694.1	pension liabilities*...........	$1,070.0
Fixed assets..................	975.2	Current liabilities.............	359.5
		Long-term debt...............	592.0
		Stockholders' equity...........	69.3
		Total Liabilities and	
Total Assets...........	$2,090.8	Stockholders' Equity....	$2,090.8

* Note: The present value of this obligation no doubt would be substantially greater if one were to use the risk-free rate as the discount rate applied to the gross vested liability.

stockholders' equity downward (by $648.5 million) to reflect the difference between the market value of the pension fund and the present value of the pension obligation. The shrinkage in the equity section of the balance sheet is striking; nearly 90 percent of the market value of the company on 12/31/75 was accounted for by the unfunded vested pension obligation. Moreover, the debt-to-equity ratio rises from 0.48 to 1 in Figure 4–2 to 0.82 to 1 in Figure 4–3 and finally to 8.5 to 1 in Figure 4–4. The augmented balance sheet illustrates the considerable increase in leverage that results if pension obligations are treated like conventional corporate liabilities.

The framework of the augmented balance sheet enables us to understand why, for many weak companies with poorly funded pension plans, the pension claim can be worth much less than its face value. Because the market value of the underlying assets is inadequate, the face value of the pension claim overstates its true economic value. Because a key element is still missing, however, this framework does not yet enable us to determine the value the economic worth of a pension claim. The next chapter supplies the missing element.

Chapter 5

What are pension claims really worth?

A cynic might describe the corporate pension fund as a financial institution whose liabilities exceed its assets. After all, few corporate pension funds are overfunded, and most are underfunded. But because the value of an institution's liabilities cannot exceed the value of its assets, it is clear that this description is absurd.[1] Despite the widespread presence in pension agreements of provisions to the effect that claimants are restricted to assets in the corporate pension fund, the corporation is obliged to make contributions sufficient to meet those claims falling due so long as it is able. There is, of course, a wide variety of actuarial funding schemes whereby the employer funds those pension benefits not yet due. But regardless of the funding scheme, the employer is required to make up any shortfall in current benefits.

Thus the difference between pension benefits and conventional lenders' claims on the employer corporation is not that the latter are empowered to reach the corporate assets and the former are not. Rather, the distinction is that conventional lenders can force the employer into bankruptcy to protect the value of their claims, whereas the pension beneficiary must wait until his or her benefits fall due. This distinction is far from unimportant. (As we shall

---

[1] Actually, the accountants have not yet decided whether, under generally accepted accounting principles, a pension fund's liabilities can exceed its assets. Under ERISA, the plan must file audited financial statements, so the accountants must address the issue. See Financial Accounting Standards Board, "An Analysis of Issues Related to Accounting and Reporting for Employee Benefit Plans," FASB Discussion Memorandum, October 6, 1975.

show, the fact that pension beneficiaries cannot reach corporate assets until their claims fall due greatly reduces the value of their claims.) Nevertheless, pension plans make financial sense only when analyzed in the context of the employer's balance sheet.

When the claim falls due, the beneficiaries get the face value of their claim or the sum of the net worth of the employer and the market value of the pension fund, whichever is less.[2] In effect, the pension beneficiaries' claims are *optioned:* they get the face value of their claims if the combined value of the underlying assets is more than the face value, or the underlying assets if the combined value of the underlying assets is less. In the latter case the employer "puts" those assets to the pension beneficiaries in return for the face value of their claims.

The point of viewing pension claims in these terms is that it reduces any pension claim to two elements, each of which can be analyzed in terms of conventional financial theory: (1) the pension claim itself, discounted at the riskless rate (as described in the previous chapter) —the so-called gross value of the claim; and (2) the so-called pension put on the corporate and pension assets underlying the claim, with a "striking price" equal to the gross value of the claim.

Clearly, the difficult part of assessing the "net value" of a pension claim is assessing the value of the pension put. Fortunately, financial scholars have developed a theory of option values that enables us to make this assessment. This book is not the place for a full-fledged exposition of this extraordinarily elegant and powerful theory. It does, however, contain an Appendix sketching out the bare bones of modern option theory and providing the valuation formulas necessary to put the theory to work.[3] In this chapter we will content ourselves with (*a*) a brief review of how options work, (*b*) a consideration of the broad factors affecting option values, and (*c*) an application of these considerations to the pension problem.

In any problem that contains an option element, that element can

---

[2] In other words, if pension assets were so depressed that they were insufficient to cover the current year's payments to beneficiaries, the company would make up the shortfall if it was able, with an additional transfer of cash to the pension fund. Only if the firm was also solvent would the beneficiaries get less than their claim. Prior to ERISA, there was no legal obligation for the companies to continue funding, but nearly all firms did so. For examples of the few exceptions, such as the Studebaker-Packard case, see Merton C. Bernstein, *The Future of Private Pensions* (London: Collier-Macmillan, Ltd., 1964).

[3] See Appendix E for a discussion of option theory under the Black-Scholes model.

be analyzed in terms of either a call option or a put option. Although most textbook illustrations take as their example the call option, we have chosen for reasons of exposition to analyze the pension option in terms of a put.

When you own a put option, you own the right to compel another party to buy a risky asset from you at a predetermined price called the "striking price" or "exercise price." When the value of the underlying asset exceeds the exercise price at the maturity of the option, it does not pay you to exercise the put and you will let the option expire unused. But when the value of the underlying asset at maturity is less than the exercise price, it will pay you to buy the

FIGURE 5-1

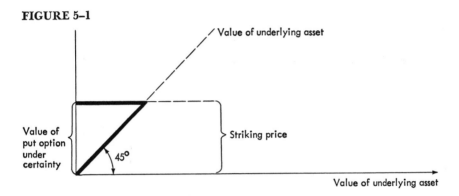

asset in the open market if you do not already own it and put it to the original seller of the option (the so-called option "writer") for the exercise price, pocketing the difference.

At the maturity of the option the relationship between the value of the option and the value of the optioned asset is easy to understand: when the underlying asset is worthless, the value of the put option is equal to its exercise price. As the value of the underlying asset increases, the value of the put option declines dollar for dollar until, when the value of the underlying asset just equals the exercise price, the put is worthless. It is also worthless for any value of the underlying asset higher than the exercise price. Thus, as a function of the underlying asset, the payoff is described by the vertical distance between the legs of the "V" outlined in Figure 5-1.

The interesting question is obviously what an option is worth that still has some time to run before maturing. Although one ex-

FIGURE 5–2

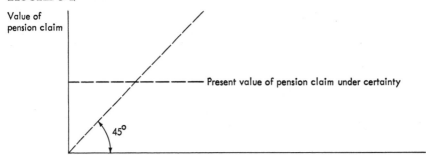

We turn now to the application of these ideas to the pension put.
pects such an option to be influenced by the value of the asset at
that time, the value of the asset at maturity is typically uncertain.
Intuition suggests that all possible values of the asset at maturity
will influence the present value of the option, and that the most
probable value of the asset will influence the present value of the
option most. When the option still has time to run, the line describing the present value of the option softens into a smooth curve,
which gets smoother and more gradually curved as time to maturity
increases. The task of option theory is to specify the precise shape of
the curve that describes the value of an option as a function of the
time remaining and the value of the underlying asset. This curve
is called the option curve.

We turn now to the application of these ideas to the pension put.
In Figures 5–2, 5–3, 5–4, and 5–5, the value of the underlying risky
asset is measured along the horizontal axis. The relevant risky asset
is the sum—in economic, or market-value, terms—of the net worth

FIGURE 5–3

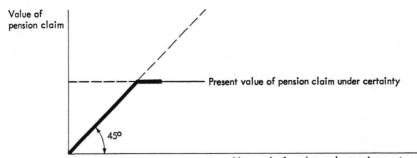

of the employer corporation and the pension assets.[4] As we shall see, there are important sets of circumstances in which pension claimants are able to reach corporate assets only if there is something left over after paying off conventional corporate creditors. For example, when the liability insurance provisions of ERISA are in effect, the Guaranty Corporation will be able to obtain contributions from the employer only until the employer's untapped borrowing power is exhausted, which will occur when corporate assets at market no longer exceed corporate liabilities. On the other hand, as long as corporate assets exceed corporate liabilities, the employer is

FIGURE 5–4

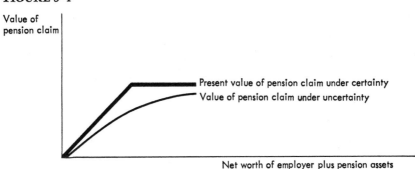

obliged to make up any shortfall in current pension benefits. Thus, despite the language in ERISA conferring on the Guaranty Corporation the power of a tax lien to reach corporate assets, the effect of liability insurance is to make the Guaranty Corporation junior for all practical purposes to corporate creditors, leaving only those corporate assets in excess of corporate liabilities available to defray the unfunded pension claims.

On the vertical axis in Figures 5–2, 5–3, 5–4, and 5–5 is measured the face value of the pension claim.[5] The 45-degree line in Figure 5–2 serves to tell us the maximum pension payoff, discounted at the riskless rate, that can be made with certainty given the value of the underlying assets. Figure 5–3 shows the value of the pension claim

---

[4] We use the net worth of the firm plus pension assets, for the reasons given in footnote 2. Thus, the pension put is a descriptive and not a legal framework for viewing the pension claim. See Appendix E for the calculation of the pension unit.

[5] The face value equals the present value of the pension claim determined on the basis of a riskless discount rate.

if there is no uncertainty about the value of the underlying asset at the time when the claim matures: it follows the 45-degree line up to its intersection with the horizontal line corresponding to the face value of the pension claim discounted at the riskless rate. As the value of the underlying assets increases beyond the point of intersection, the value of the pension claim remains unchanged.

Like the value of all options, the value of the pension put depends on the uncertainty (i.e., the dispersion in the distribution) of the optioned asset. Thus, the value to the employer corporation of the pension put increases as the uncertainty surrounding the value of these two (positively correlated) assets increases. As Figure

FIGURE 5–5

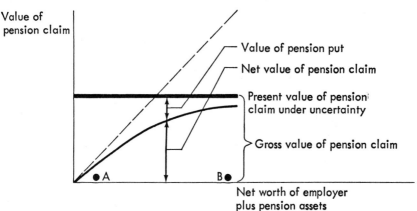

5–4 shows, if this uncertainty is made large enough, the value of the pension put can approach the value of the employer's pension liability!

Figure 5–5 shows how the value of the pension put is related to the value of the underlying assets (the sum of the net assets of the corporation proper and the pension assets) on the one hand and the pension claim on the other. As the pension claim approaches its due date the value of the claim net of the pension put approaches the kinked line shown in the figure. On the other hand, the longer until the pension claim falls due, the larger the uncertainty surrounding the value of the underlying assets at the due date, and the more gradually curved is the line describing the value of the pension put. The more gradual the curvature of the pension put, the less the pension claim net of the pension put will be worth for any given value of the underlying assets. The precise shape of this curve is specified by option theory (see Appendix E).

The pension put fairs into the 45-degree line when the underlying assets approach zero. Thus, for employers whose net assets barely exceed the amount by which their pension plan is underfunded (e.g., Point A, Figure 5–5), a loss suffered in investing in risky pension assets is borne almost entirely by pension claimants or those who have insured such risks. On the other hand, when the underlying assets are large in comparison with the face value of the pension claim (e.g., Point B), the curve describing the value of the claim net of the pension put is almost equal to the nominal value of the pension claim and parallel to it. In this circumstance, investment losses in the pension assets are borne almost entirely by the employer.

Figure 5–5 summarizes the preceding three figures, but in slightly different terms. In Figure 5–5 the face value of the pension claim discounted at the riskless rate is represented by the horizontal line called the "gross value of the pension claim." The value of the pension claim allowing for uncertainty is represented by a smooth curve called the "net value of the pension claim." The difference between the gross and net values of the pension claim is called the "value of the pension put."

Viewed this way, the pension claim is a claim against the employer rather than a claim against the pension fund, and the present value of that claim reckoned on a riskless basis represents a subtraction from the employer's equity. The pension put, on the other hand, is a claim against the pension beneficiary by the employer corporation and represents an asset of the employer.[6] If we construct an economic balance sheet for the employer corporation, it will show the pension claims as corporate liabilities (and the pension assets as corporate assets) but it will also show the put against the pension claimants as an offsetting corporate asset.

How does the preceding discussion relate to the actuary's determination of the present value of the pension liability? It is well known that the actuary's choice of the rate at which the *liability* is discounted depends in some way upon the past or future investment

---

[6] Before ERISA, the pension put was a corporate option against the plan beneficiaries. Now the put is against the insurer, with possibly a small put against the beneficiaries.

performance of the pension *asset.* Once one views the gross pension liability as a corporate liability (see the economic balance sheet in Figure 5–6), there is no more reason to single out pension liabilities for this bizarre treatment than, say, the employer's term loan with its local bank. The actuary may argue that in doing so that he or she is actually trying to estimate the value of the pension liability net of the pension put. To this rejoinder we would have three objections: (1) in order to know the value of the pension put, one has first to know the gross value of the pension liability; (2) the value of the put depends on the riskiness of the corporate assets as well as the riskiness of the pension assets; and (3) in any case, the proper discounting technique lies in the realm of option theory, rather than conventional capital budgeting. In short, there is little justification for the present actuarial practice of discounting pension liabilities at a rate somehow related to the historical rate of return on the pension assets.

FIGURE 5–6

Economic Balance Sheet
(all entries at market value)

Assets	Liabilities
Pension assets	Pension liabilities
Corporate assets	Corporate liabilities
Pension put	Employer equity

It is useful to consider in this context the impact of a pension contribution by the employer. The effect of a contribution is always to increase the pension assets while either reducing corporate assets or increasing corporate liabilities. It is in the nature of the contribution that the reduction in the net assets of the corporation never reduces the risk in the corporate assets. In other words, corporations rarely liquidate inventory or plant to pay their pension contributions; nor do they issue stock.[7] Rather, they liquidate their cash or expand creditors' claims against themselves. Either way, the pension contribution leaves the value of the net assets—corporate and pension combined—underlying pension claims unchanged. Unless the pension assets are completely riskless, however, the pension

---

[7] There have been some exceptions. For example, on August 27, 1973, Lockheed transferred a parcel of land appraised at $9.1 million to the United California Bank in lieu of the cash payment required under the pension plan.

contribution always increases; the absolute risk characterizing the underlying assets. Thus the impact of pension contributions when pension assets are at least partly risky is always to increase the value of the pension put and reduce the net value of the pension claim. Under these circumstances an employer's contribution always increases the value of the equity shares in the employer corporation. In no sense is the pension contribution an expense to the employer as sometimes supposed.

It is now possible to understand four widely observed features of corporate pension plans prior to ERISA:

1. Why some employers often made generous pension promises in lieu of increasing current wages.
2. Why some employer corporations preferred to invest pension funds in risky assets, increasing thereby the value of the put.
3. Why most conventional corporate claimants often disregarded the pension plan in evaluating their claims, implicitly allowing for the offsetting effect of the put.
4. Why even vested beneficiaries sometimes failed to collect their full pension claims.

Chapter 6

Enter ERISA

We are now in a position to consider the impact of the Employee Retirement Income Security Act of 1974. Broadly speaking, the impact of the act is very simple. It creates an entity called the Pension Benefit Guaranty Corporation and interposes this corporation between the employer and the pension beneficiary. In effect, the Guaranty Corporation is charged with paying off the beneficiary, on the one hand, and collecting from the employer on the other. Because the Guaranty Corporation has a statutory obligation to meet pension claims as they fall due, the effect of charging it with these responsibilities is to transfer pension risk from the beneficiary to the Guaranty Corporation. Under the provisions of ERISA, there is no longer any question whether, up to fairly generous statutory limits, the pension beneficiaries will get their benefits. The old question, "Will the employee get his or her benefits?" is replaced by a new question: "Who will bear the burden?" In the stead of the beneficiary, the pension act has placed a new government agency with enormous powers—the Pension Benefit Guaranty Corporation. As the law currently reads, the Guaranty Corporation has the power to reach beyond the assets in a company pension fund to the assets of the sponsoring company itself.[1] This power represents a potential revolution in the significance of pension liabilities for pension sponsors. However, one of the most important muddles in the pension act is the introduction, in parallel with the enormous powers

[1] According to Section 4062 of ERISA, the PBGC can recover from the plan sponsor an amount equal to as much as 30 percent of its "net worth." However, net worth is not clearly defined and is to be increased by "the amount of any transfers of assets made by the employer determined by the PBGC to be improper under the circumstances."

granted to the Guaranty Corporation, of the concept of liability insurance, under which insured pension sponsors can protect their
company assets from the depredations of the Guaranty Corporation.[2]
If the liability insurance provisions become a permanent feature of
the act, the great power of the Guaranty Corporation will go for
naught: Insured companies—which is to say virtually all companies
sponsoring pension plans—will be liable only to the extent of the
assets in their pension funds, putting the sponsoring companies right
back where they were before the pension act as regards responsibility
for vested benefits. (To make matters worse, the act significantly
expands the magnitude of vested benefits for most sponsors.)

The key question then becomes whether the Guaranty Corporation, obligated by law to pay these benefits, can extract enough
money from employer companies to keep from going broke. If, prior
to ERISA, some beneficiaries had difficulty collecting on their
benefits, there are at least grounds for a priori suspicion that the
Guaranty Corporation might encounter the same kind of difficulty.

Under the act, the employer is required to fund pension claims as
they are incurred and amortize unfunded past-service claims over
30 or 40 years. If the employer goes bankrupt while some fraction of
the plan's pension liability is still unfunded then, under the liability
insurance provisions of the act, the Guaranty Corporation would get
essentially nothing. More generally, under liability insurance, the
Guaranty Corporation would get the face value of the due claim or
whatever the employer is able to pay—the sum of the employer's
corporate equity and the value of the corporate pension fund, whichever is less. In effect, if the employer's resources exceed the claim, the
employer pays the claim; whereas, if the claim exceeds the employer's resources, the resources are "put" to the Guaranty Corporation in return for cancellation of the claim. In short, the effect of
the liability insurance provision of the act is to preserve intact the
pension put, greatly reducing the value to the Guaranty Corporation
of its claims on employers with pension plans.

Figure 6–1 displays the balance sheet relationships among the employer, the Guaranty Corporation (or PBGC), and the pension
beneficiary under ERISA. The employer's balance sheet has the
same items (though possibly different entry values) as it had prior
to ERISA: the pension liability, the pension assets, and the pension

---

[2] The system of contingent liability insurance is scheduled to become operable by
September 1977, according to Section 4023 of ERISA.

FIGURE 6–1

General financial relationships under ERISA

EMPLOYER

Assets	Liabilities
Corporate assets	Corporate liabilities
Pension assets	Gross pension liabilities
Pension put	Employer equity

PBGC

Assets	Liabilities
Receipts from insurance premiums	Guaranteed pension liabilities
Gross pension liabilities	Pension put
	PBGC equity, if any

BENEFICIARY

Assets	Liabilities
Guaranteed pension liabilities	

1. All entries are valued at market except the pension put—the value of which is based on option theory.
2. Both employer equity and PBGC equity are derived figures.
3. Because of the 30 percent rule, the PBGC asset, "Gross pension liabilities" will not quite equal the employer liability, "Gross pension liabilities"; similarly, the PBGC liability, "pension put," is somewhat smaller than the employer asset, "pension put," for the employee still bears a small pension put to the extent the employee has unfunded vested pension benefits that are not yet guaranteed.

put. The Guaranty Corporation has the employer's pension liability and the pension put on *its* balance sheet (but, of course, on the reverse sides) *plus* a liability to the pension beneficiary equal in amount to the employer's liability.

The balance sheet relationships of Figure 6–1 are certainly illuminating. The traditional employer balance sheet is stated in market value terms as described in Chapter 4. It has been augmented by the addition of the pension fund assets at market and pension fund liabilities in present value terms. An additional financial asset described in Chapter 5 is also present—the "pension put." While the reader may argue the absolute value of this put, the principle at work is clear. The corporation does have the option of putting its pension liability to the PBGC, and all financial options have value.[3] To the extent that this "value" exists, corporate assets are increased along with the employer's equity.

Let us now look at the PBGC and the plan beneficiary. The plan beneficiary has an asset which is equal to the employer's pension liability. ERISA has made this claim, historically somewhat ephemeral, a real asset for the beneficiary and similarly a real liability for the PBGC. In addition to this liability borne by the PBGC, there is an additional one, the pension put. Since it is a financial asset for the employer corporation, it is a financial liability for the PBGC. The combination of these two liabilities for the PBGC absolutely dwarfs its assets; these assets consist of the claim on the employers' balance sheets which are approximately equal to but most likely less than the employers' pension fund liability and the dollar per head insurance payments to be received from private pension plan sponsors. In short, using this descriptive framework, the PBGC is insolvent.

What is the magnitude of the claims against the PBGC? In the absence of contingent liability insurance, we estimate the potential claims against the PBGC at something in excess of $2 billion. But if the PBGC offers contingent liability insurance, the potential claims might rise tenfold or even thirtyfold. In July 1975, *Dun's Review* published a list of the 30 companies with the largest unfunded

---

[3] As an example of how real this option is, suppose Lockheed had terminated its pension plan at the end of 1974. The liability for unfunded vested benefits, which was $420 million, would have been "put" to the PBGC. The latter would have then attached a lien equal to 30 percent of Lockheed's net worth, or $8 million. Hence, at the end of 1974, Lockheed had a put option against the PBGC which was worth some $412 million. This option was surely an asset for Lockheed.

vested pension liabilities in relation to stockholder's equity.[4] Sixteen of the firms had unfunded vested liabilities that exceeded 30 percent of net worth. If each of them had terminated its pension plan at the end of 1974 and if the PBGC had guaranteed the amount by which the unfunded vested benefits exceed 30 percent of net worth, the PBGC would have been short nearly $2 billion, as it could have recovered only $3 billion of the $5 billion in total unfunded vested benefits. Furthermore, "net worth" is not clearly defined in Section 4062 of the act, and because all of the companies were selling far below book value, they might have argued (as we have argued in previous chapters) that the net worth calculation should be on a market basis instead of a book basis.[5] But on a market valuation basis, the PBGC would have been stuck with $4 billion of the $5 billion liability for unfunded vested benefits.

The *Dun's Review* survey included the 400 or so corporations that had 1974 sales of at least $400 million. Because only 16 of them were over the 30-percent-of-net-worth mark, we can conclude that without contingent liability insurance, an estimated 5 percent of the major corporations have an economic claim against the PBGC, and that the total claims amount to several billion dollars.

With contingent liability insurance, nearly all unfunded vested benefits would be guaranteed, probably by the PBGC. The government has never published an estimate of total unfunded vested benefits, but the figure is probably between $20 billion and $60 billion.[6]

---

[4] Arlene Hershman, "The Big Pension Fund Drain," *Dun's Review,* July 1975, pp. 31–35.

[5] Section 4062 states that net worth should be determined on "whatever basis best reflects, in the determination of the Guaranty Corporation, the curren status of the employer's operations and prospects at the time chosen for determining the net worth of the employer."

[6] The 40 companies in our survey had $27.4 billion in pension assets, the equivalent of 20 percent of the book value and 25 percent of the market value of the assets held by all private, noninsured pension plans. If the $12 billion unfunded vested liability of the 40 companies was also representative of the universe, the unfunded vested liability of the entire pension system was between $48 billion and $60 billion. Our survey indicated that the average company had an unfunded vested liability equal to 5 percent of stockholder's equity. Applying the 5 percent rate to the Federal Trade Commission's estimate of $408 billion in stockholder's equity for all manufacturing corporations at the end of 1974, we arrive at a $20 billion estimate of total unfunded vested benefits. In its June 16, 1975, issue, *Business Week* reported that its survey of 200 leading corporations showed $16 billion in unfunded vested benefits and $30 billion in unfunded past-service costs. Taken together, the figures indicate total unfunded vested benefits were probably in the $20 to $60 billion range at the end of 1974.

Can the PBGC afford to increase its risk by this amount? That depends on how well it can absorb claims. In 1975, the PBGC built up a $35 million reserve from the money it collected in premiums, based on a levy of 50 cents per participant in multiemployer plans and $1 per participant for all others. But the reserve was strained by 5,500 plan terminations in the first year of ERISA.[7] This was four times as many terminations as the PBGC had expected, and more than three fourths of the plans were under funded at the termination date. Steven Schanes, the first executive director of the PBGC, noted that "perhaps 700 are real problem cases in which we will have really heavy responsibilities. This is much higher than anticipated."[8] The largest termination in 1975 was the Diamond Reo Truck Company, which went bankrupt and left a pension plan with $5 million in assets and $21 million in liabilities. Clearly, the PBGC's $35 million fund cannot sustain many terminations of that size and still remain viable.

When *Forbes* magazine asked Schanes how the PBGC planned to handle the large number of terminations, he responded, "The Pension Benefit Guaranty Corporation is to be self-supporting, so we may have to go back and revise our rates." But he added that, "Obviously, we can't suddenly say, 'Hey fellas, we guessed wrong. Everybody cough up three times last year's premiums.'"[9]

Schanes was discussing the premium schedule without contingent liability insurance, implying that the $35 million fund was not sufficient to insure the $2 billion or so of potential claims. If the premium for basic coverage was tripled, and that figure was increased twentyfold to allow for contingent liability insurance, the total premium would be $60 per participant, an incredible jump from the original $1 levy. Even worse, the company with no unfunded vested liability would receive nothing in return for the higher premium. For example, with a quarter of a million employees and a $60 premium, Chrysler would pay about $15 million annually to insure its $1.2 billion unfunded vested liability. But J. C. Penney, with nearly 200,000 employees, would pay about $12 million in premiums but receive little or no insurance coverage, because it had no unfunded

---

[7] Ernest Dickinson, "Backing Out of Paying Pensions," *New York Times,* February 8, 1976.

[8] "Too Much Business?" *Forbes,* October 15, 1975.

[9] Ibid.

vested benefits at the end of 1974. It would make sense for a low-risk company like Penney to turn to private insurers and pay a lower premium, but Section 4023 of ERISA states that if the PBGC develops a system of contingent liability insurance that involves private insurers, the PBGC "shall devise a system under which risks are equitably distributed between the Corporation and private insurers with respect to the classes of employers insured by each."[10] In other words, the PBGC does not intend to insure only the high-risk companies while the private sector handles the low-risk situations. Only by requiring mandatory participation and setting moderate premium schedules can the PBGC hope to spread the risk among the strong and the weak companies.

One way the PBGC hopes to spread the risk is through portfolio diversification. The main difference between the Guaranty Corporation under ERISA and the pension beneficiary prior to ERISA is the fact that the Guaranty Corporation is holding a portfolio of claims on many thousands of pension plans. Thus the Guaranty Corporation's portfolio will be highly diversified whether or not individual pension portfolios are diversified. On the other hand, the level of market risk in the Guaranty Corporation's portfolio will be the average of the levels of market risk in the individual pension portfolios. No amount of diversification in individual pension portfolios will eliminate the market risk in the Guaranty Corporation's portfolio. Thus, when losses arise, the Guaranty Corporation is likely to find itself faced with losses in a great many pension plans simultaneously. In the end, because its portfolio contains claims on thousands of individual pension funds, diversification in the individual pension portfolio is almost worthless. It is hard to see how the diversification provisions of ERISA can accomplish their intended purpose.

Since the impact on the Guaranty Corporation's equity of the pension liability from the employer to the Guaranty Corporation is equal and opposite to the impact of the liability from the Guaranty Corporation to the beneficiary, the net effect of the pension plan is to reduce the Guaranty Corporation's equity by the value of the pension put. As noted, the value of the pension put is typically of the same order of magnitude as, although smaller than, the pension

[10] Section 4023 (a) of ERISA.

liability itself. In aggregate terms, therefore, the consequence of liability insurance (which, as noted, perpetuates the pension put) is a charge against the Guaranty Corporation's equity of some tens of billions of dollars. If the liability insurance feature of ERISA survives, this charge will grow rapidly.

It should be apparent from these comments that with the liability insurance provisions of the act intact, ERISA preserves the position of the employer company virtually unchanged from what it was prior to the new legislation. It still pays some employers to make pension promises that they may not be able to honor. And, despite the elaborate fiduciary responsibility provisions in the act, it still pays some employers to encourage managers of their pension funds to manage them aggressively. One can conjecture, however, that if the Guaranty Corporation fails, the pension fund manager will be made the goat on grounds of having failed to fulfill his or her "fiduciary responsibility."

To sum up our main conclusions to this point: (*a*) The Pension Act of 1974 makes pension claims genuine claims. (*b*) It establishes a quasi-governmental agency, the Guaranty Corporation, charged with making sure the claims get paid. (*c*) It gives the Guaranty Corporation enormous power to reach the assets of the sponsoring companies—unless those companies have liability insurance. (*d*) Liability insurance may or may not help smooth the transition from the old game, under which pension liabilities were simply numbers on a piece of paper, to the new game legislated by the act, under which the company's pension liabilities are as real as its bank debt and considerably more senior. But it encourages sponsoring companies to pursue investment programs that are risk oriented and places an insupportable burden on the Guaranty Corporation.

Part 3

Implications and advice for the game players

Chapter 7

Implications and advice for the game players

Whose money is at risk? This is a key question for the Guaranty Corporation; lenders to the employer; the employer's shareholders, the managers of the pension portfolio, who may be called on to advise on the risk objectives of the portfolio; and security analysts.

The answer to this question, although provided by Chapter 5, is not as simple as one might like: in the absence of liability insurance it is primarily the employer's money that is at stake because there is no "pension put."[1] On the other hand, with liability insurance the employer shoulders the burden if the pension plan is strong (i.e., small pension put) but the insurer bears the burden if the pension plan is weak (i.e., large pension put). In between these extremes is a gray area in which the way the risk is shared between the employer and the insurer is constantly shifting with the changing fortunes of the employer and its pension plan.

Since there is an important element of systematic or market risk in the fortunes of most employers and virtually all pension portfolios, the risk that the insurer bears cannot be entirely diversified away; the insurer will find that many, if not most, of the employers being insured will get into trouble at about the same time.[2] Ignoring for the moment the fact that there are a number of ways in which

---

[1] To the extent the unfunded vested liability is less than 30 percent of net worth, the burden would be solely that of the employer corporation.

[2] Systematic or market risk is that portion of total risk that cannot be diversified away; it is that portion of risk unique to the asset class. On average, one third of the price fluctuations of a one-stock portfolio can be traced to general market price movements, with the remaining risk reflecting factors peculiar to the industry and the

the insured employer can increase the insurer's risk exposure more or less at will, the fact that the so-called contingent liability risk in the pension system cannot be diversified away itself guarantees that sooner or later anyone who undertakes to insure this risk will likely be bankrupted by it.

THE GUARANTY CORPORATION

This question of insuring market risk is obviously an important one for any private firm that would undertake to provide this type of insurance, but it is also important for employer corporations who might undertake to rely on such insurers and for the Guaranty Corporation. If employers rely on private insurers they will find that just when they need their contingent liability insurance, the insurer is likely to be insolvent and the insurance worthless. Deprived of the proceeds of their insurance at a time when they are unable to meet their pension obligations, many employer companies will lack sufficient net worth to permit the Guaranty Corporation to bail itself out. It follows that even if private insurers were foolish enough to offer this kind of insurance, both employer companies and the Guaranty Corporation itself would have a big stake in finding a better way.[3]

Unfortunately, under ERISA only one other way is available—that is, for the Guaranty Corporation (PBGC) to become the universal insurer. But, if this is done, the PBGC will not become involved until the "insurance" is needed. Thus, despite the language in the act conferring on the PBGC the power of a "tax lien," its role as insurer will prevent it from acting until the employer company is conventionally bankrupt—effectively making the Guaranty Corporation junior to all other conventional corporate creditors.

Furthermore, it is clear that while any given plan may be poorly diversified, all plans collectively are highly diversified. In effect the risk exposure of the PBGC is market risk. Given that the PBGC will

---

particular company. As more securities are added to the portfolio, specific industry and company influences account for less and less of the total risk in the portfolio. Thus, in a large, diversified institutional portfolio, the total risk in the portfolio is almost entirely market risk.

[3] It is worth noting in the pending bill, HR7597, the insurance industry was successful in changing the phrase whereby the PBGC "shall" devise a system under which the risks are equitably distributed between the PBGC and private insurers, to "may" devise a system.

have some assets to meet these liabilities, how should they be invested? Obviously, the PBGC will be under the greatest pressure when the general economy is performing poorly. If the liabilities are going to be subject to overall economic risk, the assets funding these liabilities should not be exposed to the same kind of risk. Indeed, one can argue that these assets should be riskless in character. Yet the PBGC is embarking on the opposite path. It has hired several asset managers to invest assets of terminated plans in the same kind of securities held by the run-of-the-mill pension fund. In short, the PBGC will be attempting to offset market risk with market risk, a self-defeating strategy. One can easily envision the case where the PBGC's liability is rising at the same time the assets expected to offset this liability are shrinking in value.

Knowing *when* the Guaranty Corporation will act is of interest to all the game players. In addition to the perverse effect of liability insurance, a second major section of the act bears scrutiny—particularly in the event liability insurance is expunged from the act. In attempting to meet its claims, the PBGC can place a lien on the employer corporation's net assets to the extent of 30 percent in the event of plan termination. "Net worth" apparently means "equity," but in market value terms rather than accounting or book value terms. For example, it is hard to believe the PBGC could obtain 30 percent of the book value of Wheeling Pittsburgh Steel when the market value of the entire company approximates 20 percent of book.

If the Guaranty Corporation waits until a company is bankrupt in the conventional sense to force involuntary termination, the "net worth" of the company will be roughly zero. Because 30 percent of zero is still zero, despite the fact that its claim on the company's assets has the power of a tax lien, the Guaranty Corporation will get virtually nothing from the company's assets with which to defray its pension liability (e.g., W. T. Grant).

On the other hand, the act charges the Guaranty Corporation with the responsibility of enforcing involuntary termination whenever its risk begins to increase "unreasonably." That point is clearly reached long before conventional bankruptcy. In order to be able to defray the unfunded liability with the proceeds of its claim on the company's assets, the Guaranty Corporation must force involuntary termination while 30 percent of the company's net assets still exceeds the unfunded pension liability—which is to say, while the company's net assets still exceed 3.3 times the unfunded pension liability. This becomes the critical number for the Guaranty Corporation.

If the 30 percent provision is to protect the net assets against the claims of the Guaranty Corporation, the Guaranty Corporation must wait until the company is conventionally bankrupt. Will it do so? Or will it act soon enough to recover from the terminating company's assets the value of the unfunded pension liability? In view of the fact that it has both the power to terminate a pension plan and the responsibility to terminate "before the risk to its own assets begins to increase unreasonably," can there be any doubt how the Guaranty Corporation should behave?

With or without the liability insurance features of the pension act, the Guaranty Corporation needs to know the status of individual pension plans with far more accuracy than is possible from conventional actuarial and accounting reports. As explained in Chapter 5, with liability insurance many employers will in fact hold substantial "puts" against the Guaranty Corporation. (Without liability insurance some employers will still have "puts" to the extent the unfunded vested benefits exceeds 30 percent of net assets at market.) In order to know its own financial position, the Guaranty Corporation needs to be able to estimate the value and the magnitude of these puts for it is in its own interest to limit the size of the corporate "pension put." For this purpose information not only about the individual pension plan but also about the sponsoring corporation is essential.

Reporting of individual pension plans needs to be uniform. The value of all pension assets should be determined at the same time and in the same way, and pension liabilities reckoned on the basis of uniform mortality tables and uniform discount rates. In addition the Guaranty Corporation needs up-to-date information on any changes in the employer's capital structure and in policies according to which pension assets are invested.

Finally, the PBGC needs to recognize that corporate dividend policy directly affects the value of the pension put against the Guaranty Corporation for a dollar paid in dividends reduces the value of the assets underlying the pension claim by a like amount. Hence, the Guaranty Corporation needs the authority to limit dividend payments by the weak employer with a weak pension plan.[4]

---

[4] Depending upon interpretation, this authority may already exist as a result of Section 4062.

THE EMPLOYER COMPANY

ERISA presents the employer corporation with a difficult situation: If the liability insurance feature of the act becomes operational, the financially weak employer—taking corporation and pension plan together—bears a relatively small share of the investment risk in the pension portfolio. If the liability insurance features are deleted from the act, however, the burden of risk in the pension portfolio and increased pension promises will be borne entirely by the employer—precisely as if pension liabilities were corporate liabilities and pension assets were corporate assets.[5] In a sense it behooves the weak employer corporation to take advantage of the pension put—to make generous pension promises and to manage its pension portfolio aggressively. Once Congress understands the problem for the Guaranty Corporation that liability insurance creates, there is a fair chance that it will act to delete this feature from the act, leaving high and dry those companies that made excessively generous pension promises on the assumption that the Guaranty Corporation would end up paying the tab. Such companies may have occasion to regret doing so.

Regarding the appropriate policy for a corporate pension fund, it has been advocated that the investment policy should reflect the total nature of the firm, including its industry role, life cycle position, cyclicality of business, age mix of the work force, financial status of the company, and the retirement plan as well as a host of other factors. Hence, a firm like IBM with a rental revenue base, an above-average growth rate, a well-funded plan, and a relatively young work force can afford to adopt a high-risk policy in its pension fund.

Over time it can be shown that higher risk almost always results in higher returns (e.g., common stocks outperform bonds). Thus, a strong firm can afford to bear the interim volatility of a risk oriented investment policy in hopes of achieving the longer term higher return. But a mature company in a mature industry with an old work force and weak financial position cannot bear the short-term volatility of a high-risk policy. Hence, its investment strategy should be oriented away from high-risk securities (i.e., equities).

ERISA, with its liability insurance provision, alters this line of reasoning. Other corporate objectives aside, weak companies (those with large pension puts) can have high-risk investment policies.

---

[5] To the extent the UVB is less than 30 percent of net worth.

This results from the fact that the company bears less risk if results are unsuccessful and benefits to a greater extent if results are favorable. In other words, the risk/return tradeoff is not a straight line relationship and the curve is biased in favor of the company and against the PBGC (see Figure 5–5 of Chapter 5).

Under ERISA the strong company has no more to gain than lose, however, by pursuing a high-risk investment policy. The strong company will have a large net worth at market, and its plan will be well funded in the sense described in this book. Hence its "pension put" is quite small, and a dollar loss in pension assets will be borne at a rate almost dollar for dollar by the shareholder.

In order to formulate the proper investment policy, a corporation should first construct an augmented balance sheet as described in Chapter 4 and determine if it is a strong or weak company. If strong, the economic balance sheet, with its pension put, will be almost the same as the augmented balance sheet because the put is so small that it does not have to be considered. If weak, then the pension put should be estimated as described in Appendix E. An appropriate risk policy for the pension fund evolves from this analysis, but changes may be required to reflect shifts in the financial position of the firm.

ERISA also creates complications for the employer companies contemplating mergers or acquisitions. So long as the liability insurance feature is operating, the merger of the strong employer with the weak one will negate much of the value of the weak employer's pension put for the put is transferred from the Guaranty Corporation to the strong partner; through the merger the claim against the PBGC becomes a claim against the strong partner. In the absence of liability insurance, of course, companies contemplating merger or acquisition should evaluate acquisition prospects, treating pension assets and liabilities as corporate assets and liabilities, respectively.[6]

THE LENDERS

The implications for the lender are now evident. With liability insurance it makes a great deal of difference to lenders whether the

---

[6] For example, Kennecott Copper is required to divest itself of Peabody Coal. The purchaser may be required to assume an unfunded pension liability which in effect reduces the value of Peabody to it. Interestingly enough, a weak company can pay more for Peabody than a strong one since the Peabody pension put will remain against the PBGC for the former whereas it would be netted against the equity of the strong firm. Although the Peabody example involves a multiemployer plan where the employer might have to make additional contributions to cover an unfunded liability, the principle is the same for a corporate pension plan.

insurer is a private company or the Guaranty Corporation. If the employer to whom the lender is lending gets into trouble at a time when other employers are pressuring a private insurer to collect insurance benefits, the employer may receive no insurance proceeds with which to cover the unfunded pension liability. If it chooses to force termination then, the Guaranty Corporation will of course be restricted to 30 percent of the employer's net worth—presumably on an economic rather than a book basis—but to that extent at least its claim will be senior to those of any private lender.

On the other hand if, as seems likely, the insurer ultimately becomes the Guaranty Corporation, then the effect of liability insurance is to prevent it from reaching any corporate assets whatsoever. In this case, private lenders are effectively senior to the Guaranty Corporation, which in turn has little to gain in these circumstances from forcing termination.

In the absence of liability insurance, the Guaranty Corporation, as previously noted, is senior to unsecured lenders. This is, however, no reason for despair on the part of the latter.

To be sure, because the value of the pension portfolio influences the unfunded liability, these fluctuations can influence the likelihood and timing of the forced termination. But forced termination by the PBGC can strengthen, rather than weaken, the position of the private creditor since the Guaranty Corporation must act long before conventional bankruptcy to protect itself (in fact, it must act when the net worth at market of the company is equal to $3\frac{1}{3}$ times its claim). In addition to the volatility of the firm itself, the lender is interested in knowing the volatility of the pension fund. A volatile funding policy can also increase the lender's risk for it means the unfunded vested benefit claim can swing widely.

Finally, the lender to an employer corporation needs to be aware that if the liability insurance provisions of the pension act are expunged, the sensitivity of the lender's claim to fluctuations in the general prosperity will be sharply increased. If the quality of the claim is sufficiently high, this increase will be of no significance to the lender. On the other hand, it may be of great significance if the loan was marginal to begin with.

THE SHAREHOLDERS

We have explained why, in certain circumstances, pension liabilities have so little net value as to be a negligible burden to the employer corporation. There are circumstances where the pension put is operating—that is, either before ERISA, or after ERISA but with liability insurance—and where the value of the augmented assets exceeds the gross value of claims (including pension claims) by a margin narrow compared to the uncertainty variance surrounding the future value of the assets at the time the pension claims mature. In these combinations of circumstances, the investment analyst can ignore the pension plan in assessing the shares of the employer company. But this does not mean that the continuing student of the company's shares can ignore the pension plan:

1. Circumstances change. The company may prosper, widening the margin between assets and claims, or the riskiness of the combined corporate and pension assets may diminish. In either case, the value of the pension put will diminish, and the burden of the pension plan net of the pension put will increase. Even if the burden was negligible before, it may be negligible no longer.

2. Indeed, whereas in the case of normal claims against the company, losses and gains in the value of its assets are borne almost entirely by shareholders, in the case just described, they are borne primarily by the pension claimants before ERISA and by the PBGC after.

3. In particular, a new equity issue will add primarily to the value of the company's pension claims rather than to the value of its equity. Thus the old shareholders will find the number of shares increased by the issue without a commensurate increase in the aggregate equity, and the value of their old shares consequently diminished.

4. On the other hand, a company whose augmented assets exceed its liabilities (including pension obligations) by a margin wide in comparison to the variance surrounding the future value of the assets at the time the pension claims mature has a negligible pension put. Thus the value of its equity is reduced by virtually the full amount of its (unfunded) pension liability—even though the pension put is operating.

5. When the pension put is operating, therefore, it is not possible to generalize about who bears the burden of investment losses in the pension portfolio: the shareholder bears them if the company is sufficiently strong, and the Guaranty Corporation bears them if the company is sufficiently weak.

6. Neither, when the pension put is operating, can one generalize

about the impact of an increase in pension liabilities. The shareholder bears virtually the full impact of the gross value of the liabilities when the company is strong, but hardly any impact when the company is weak.

7. When, on the other hand, the pension put is not operating, the impact of the pension plan is precisely as if both pension assets and pension liabilities were on the corporate balance sheet. Gains and losses in the market value of the pension portfolio will, in a reasonably efficient capital market, be translated immediately into equal changes in the aggregate market value of the employer's own shares. Increases in the present value of the pension liability will be translated into equal reductions in the aggregate value of the employer's shares. And, for this purpose, the market will reckon the present value of the pension liability by discounting "expected" (i.e., on basis of actuarial probabilities) future obligations at the riskless rate.

It is worth noting that many companies with pension funds will be holding each other's common stock in their pension portfolios. When the market value of these companies goes down, the value of the pension portfolio holding shares in these companies goes down. When pension liabilities are corporate liabilities and pension assets corporate assets, then a drop in the value of the corporate pension portfolio will cause the value of the corporate market shares to fall —and the whole cycle will begin all over again. The cycle will continue until the whole process finally converges at some much lower value for the pension portfolios and some much lower value for the shares of the corporations owning the portfolios. Thus a one dollar drop in the conventionally reckoned ("old") equity of the representative corporation will ultimately cause the value of its shares reckoned on an augmented basis (the "new" equity) to drop by more than one dollar. The factor by which one multiplies the change in the value of the former to obtain the resulting change in the value of the latter is termed the "pension multiplier."

The relationship between the "old" equity and the "new" equity is shown in the following T account. If we let e equal the old equity,

Old equity	Pension liability	(1)
Pension asset	New equity	

a the value of the pension portfolio, l the present value of the vested pension liability, and e' the new equity, then we can write

$$e' = e + a - l$$

where the old equity, the pension asset, and the new equity are all measured in terms of current market value.

Under specific conditions it can be shown that the pension multiplier is equal to:

$$\frac{1}{1 - \dfrac{l}{e}} \tag{2}$$

As the symbols have been defined, this particularly simple result holds only for the special case in which pension assets are invested entirely in the equity shares of companies with similarly situated pension plans. More generally, however, the same equation can be adapted to two other situations: (1) If only part of the pension fund is invested in equities, and the remainder in debt, the debt portion can be viewed as an offset to the pension liability. In other words, interpret l as the pension liability net of the debt portion of the pension portfolio, and a as the equity portion of the pension portfolio. Then the same result holds.

Again, if only part of the equity portion of the typical pension portfolio is invested in shares of companies which themselves have pension portfolios, that part can be viewed as an extension of the old equity. In other words, interpret e as the sum of the old equity and the portion of the pension portfolio invested in shares of companies without pension plans and a as the remainder. Applied in this way, Equation 2 still holds.

As pointed out, this argument is only valid when the portfolio holds equities of corporations with similar pension situations. This is true more often than not when one examines the concentration of the names of equities in the typical portfolio and the concentration of asset management of these portfolios.

Almost of necessity there will be a great deal of concentration. This is reflected in Table 6–1 where the book value of shareholders' equity is shown for the 1,000 largest manufacturing corporations as of December 31, 1974.[7]

This table illustrates the concentration of industry. The 500 largest companies comprise 91 percent of the book value of the 1,000 largest industrial companies, and the 10 leading firms are nearly 25 percent of the net worth of these 1,000 companies. In other words,

---

[7] *Fortune,* May and June 1975.

1 percent of the largest 1,000 industrial firms account for 25 percent of the net worth of these same corporations.

This trend is reflected in the market value of equities as well. The largest index of companies weighted by common shares outstanding is the Wilshire 5,000 stock index which had a 1974 year-end value of $586.0 billion, and the 20 largest holdings accounted for 42 percent of this index's value.

When one looks at who manages these assets, one finds again large concentration. There are 14,000 commercial banks in the United States, and about 3,800 have trust powers, but the largest 100 hold 85 percent of trust assets. The business is heavily concentrated in New York where the 10 largest of these 3,800 banks have

TABLE 6–1

Book Value of Corporate Shareholders' Equity
December 1974
($ in billions)

1,000 largest industrial companies..............	$340	preliminary
500 largest industrial companies..............	309.4	actual
10 largest industrial companies..............	77.8	actual

$114 billion in trust assets—25 percent of the nation's total. These banks tend to own the same securities. *Fortune* magazine in July 1973 provided a revealing table which displayed the 20 largest holdings of each of the 17 largest bank trust departments. On the average, the 20 largest holdings accounted for over 40 percent of the value of the total common stock position. As expected, these companies were, for the most part, the 20 largest companies in the United States (at market value) possessing a combined market value at 12/31/72 of $283 billion equal to 43.2 percent of the aggregate market value of the S & P 500 at that point in time.

In short, a small number of common stocks, as few as 50 which are under the management of 20 financial institutions, dominate the market value of the common stock holdings of private, noninsured, pension funds. Since common stocks are approximately 60 percent of the value of all uninsured pension plan assets, it is easy to see that the performance of the common stock prices of a limited number of companies possess an overwhelming influence on the outcome of the equity component of private, noninsured pension funds.[8] In other

---

[8] Securities and Exchange Commission, "Private Noninsured Pension Funds, 1974" *SEC Statistical Bulletin,* April 1975.

words, the "favorite 50" is a rather accurate proxy for the performance of the major component of pension assets.

The major point here is that the net effect of the pension multiplier is to increase the leverage of the firm whenever risky assets are used as the pension liability funding vehicle. Appendix F illustrates an example of this calculation; and although it is artificial in a number of respects for the sake of clarity of exposition, the results are highly instructive. The example focuses on 20 of the most widely held corporations in the United States and makes the extreme simplifying assumption that the portion of pension assets not devoted to each other's common stocks is entirely invested in companies with no pension plans whatsoever. Even so, the pension multiplier for this example is 1.14 on average, showing that if the pension liability became a full corporate liability the systematic or market risk in these companies' equities would increase 14 percent. In other words, because the pension assets are invested in securities of companies with their own pension plans, the volatility is increased, in this case by approximately 14 percent. For reasons detailed in Appendix F we believe this multiplier to be far lower than the true one for publicly held companies generally.

THE ASSET MANAGER

The language of the act raises many questions, but once again the key one is "Whose money is at risk?" Fund managers concerned for the safety of the bonds in their portfolio can consult "Implications for the Lender." Fund managers concerned for their common stocks can consult "Implications for the Shareholder." But this question has implications for fund managers that go beyond implications for the value or risk character for the securities in a portfolio.

What constitutes prudent behavior for the pension fiduciary is still hazy, still fluid. It is clear from the new "prudent man" language in the pension act that the old common-law tradition of *Harvard* v. *Amory* no longer rules, but precisely what the new language will mean is not yet clear.

The pension fund manager wants to avoid not merely the penalties prescribed by the act for derelict fiduciaries, but also the expense of litigation—particularly since early cases under the act are likely to be long, involved, and complex.

By placing strong emphasis on diversification, Congress no doubt believed that investment risk would be substantially eliminated. We know this is not the case because of the presence of market risk. Nevertheless, it may take one or more court cases to demonstrate that merely because an asset manager lost money, he or she was not necessarily "poorly diversified."

Because the asset manager not only wants to win any legal battle but also to avoid the expense of litigation, employers with weak pension plans may be declined service. Thus, one important task for the asset manager is to review prospective pension fund clients using the augmented and economic balance sheets. Not only will this analysis help asset managers frame an investment policy but it will also be of assistance in identifying desirable clients.

One final comment relates to the asset manager and the desire for protection under ERISA's fiduciary standards. Nearly all employee benefit fund managers, either at the request of their clients or on their own, have sought fiduciary liability insurance. Unfortunately, this insurance is likely to be as useless for the manager as contingent liability insurance is for the PBGC.

Many of these policies contain language that indicates that losses "arising as a result of failures to act prudently under ERISA" will be covered. Nevertheless, these policies have exclusions covering acts under which the insurance company will not pay. Two of these are of special note and can be construed to cover a multiple of sins:

1. Any intentional noncompliance with any statute or regulation.
2. Alleged excessive or unwarranted investment management or advisory fees or charges, or excessive or unwarranted brokerage fees or commissions, or sales loads.

Frequently, the surety insurance companies that write this type of insurance do not pay claims—certainly not significant ones—when asserted. Rather they insist that all possible defenses be utilized, and that the claim be litigated, fully. Settlement occurs, if at all, on the eve of trial. As a result, the insured company finds that it must bear the very substantial burden of having its people involved in giving depositions, and all the other things that are required to assist the lawyers preparing the case for trial.

Since payment of the premium does not protect the insured (except, perhaps, from having to pay a judgment if one is obtained, or the amount of a settlement paid when trial is imminent and the case considered risky), many business people and lawyers have questioned the value of purchasing this very expensive insurance.

ANALYSTS

For security and credit analysts, the central issue is the determination of which parties bear the pension fund risk and in what proportion. The analyst cannot form a judgment until the necessary figures are collected and the actuarial methods and assumptions upon which the figures are based are examined. As we discussed in Part 1, such information is seldom disclosed in annual and 10-K reports. Hence, in management interviews, the analyst should try to obtain answers to the following questions:

1. What is the present value of total vested benefits and the market value of pension assets, as of the same valuation date? Does the net difference between these two figures correspond to the unfunded vested benefits figure in the company's annual report? Why not?
2. What are the key actuarial assumptions; how conservative are they in light of recent experience; and how do they compare to industry norms? Have they been changed recently, and what was the impact on pension costs and liabilities?
3. Have benefits been improved or a new labor contract negotiated, and what will be the impact on pension costs and liabilities?

Some of this information is available in reports filed with the U.S. Department of Labor. Under the Welfare and Pension Plans Disclosure Act of 1958, which was superceded by ERISA, corporations and other groups are required to file annual reports with the Labor Department on each of their retirement plans (and some companies have more than 100 plans) within 150 days of the end of the fiscal or calendar year. The principal document is the D-2 annual report, which describes the assets and liabilities of the plan, the cash receipts and disbursements, the valuation and funding methods, and the key actuarial assumptions. The D-1-S report describes the benefits, the vesting provisions, and the eligibility standards of the plan. Under ERISA, new forms and reports will be required.

With this information, the analyst can construct an augmented balance sheet and determine the degree of leverage introduced by the addition of the pension assets and liabilities. Then an "adjusted" debt-to-equity ratio can be computed as we did in Chapter 4.

In this framework, the analyst can see how increases in stock and bond prices can translate into a reduction of unfunded pension liabilities and, with lower amortization costs, an increase in reported earnings.

This approach also enables an analyst to assess the impact of the company closing a plant or selling a subsidiary, for the company may have to terminate the pension plan covering the affected workers and make good the unfunded vested benefits.

Another element analysts must reexamine is intermediate-term bank loans that are coming due. Because ERISA puts them in a potentially subordinated position, commercial banks may be reluctant to make or extend loans to companies with pension liability problems.

For a detailed analysis of the risk the credit analyst would be assuming as a lender, augmented balance sheets can be constructed for the last several years. Then it can be determined if there was any year in which the company's position as a creditor would have deteriorated significantly as a result of a sharp increase in the liability for unfunded vested benefits. Further research should indicate whether the increase in the UVB liability was due primarily to a decline in the market value of the pension portfolio or a major increase in benefits.

In assessing the value of the firm, the credit and the security analyst should construct an economic balance sheet with its pension put. For this purpose he can refer to Chapter 5, which describes how pension obligations affect the worth of the firm.

Epilogue

The pension system
and public policy

The ostensible purpose of the Employee Retirement Income Security Act of 1974 was to make certain that the beneficiaries got paid. This was accomplished by creating the Pension Benefit Guaranty Corporation and charging it with the responsibility to meet pension claims as they fell due (up to the statutory limit specified by the act.) Although they were tacit, however, the act had at least two other purposes:

1. To prevent pension plans from becoming wards of the public —thereby socializing the private pension system.
2. To see that the employer who receives consideration in the form of labor for its pension promises does not evade the financial responsibility for fulfilling these promises.

As we have pointed out, the liability insurance feature of ERISA defeats these tacit purposes of the act. If this feature survives, many weak employers will escape bearing a large part of their pension burden. Knowing that they have an excellent chance of escaping, they may be tempted to make more generous pension promises and to take larger risks with their pension portfolios than otherwise. In the first instance, the burden increases; and in the second, the burden shifts—in large part through the mechanism of the pension put —to the Guaranty Corporation (which is to say, the U.S. government).

Although the liability insurance feature cannot be removed from the act without increasing the financial burden on many companies —in the process, perhaps, driving some into bankruptcy—the feature should be removed at the first opportunity. The opportunity will arise when the country is sufficiently prosperous and its capital markets sufficiently strong that all but a few employer companies can bear the extra financial burden resulting from removal of this provision. Even at this point, the government is likely to have to step in and assist some pension plans, but the cost will be far smaller than the cost of permitting the pension system, flawed as it is by the liability insurance provision, to fail.

Our reasoning thus far assumes that liability insurance is unworkable. To be insurable, a risk must satisfy two basic requirements:

1. The incidence and magnitude of risk must not be under the insuree's control. Under the pension act there are two ways in which the sponsoring company can increase the likelihood that the insurer will be called on to pay off an underfunded pension plan: (*a*) The company can increase the risk in the underlying assets. As noted above, the value of the option premium depends on the riskiness of the underlying asset. Thus, not only is the company likely to have some latitude to undertake such a risk increase, it actually profits directly from doing so (unless, of course, constrained by the "fiduciary" provisions of the act). (*b*) Sponsoring companies will frequently be in labor negotiations in which there is a tradeoff between current wages and future pension benefits. To the extent that the insurer has a chance of being left holding the bag, the shareholders of the company gain by opting to increase benefits rather than wages. Every time a sponsoring company wins in this way, the insurer loses.

Sponsoring corporations will always have a considerable latitude to alter the probability of going bankrupt. If, to avoid burdening the taxpayer with the cost of supporting companies that exploit this latitude, the insurer increases the insurance "premium" imposed on strong, healthy conservative companies, it will be creating a conduit by which wealth will flow from the responsible, careful companies to the irresponsible, careless ones.

2. The risks to be insured must be poolable. The distinction between specific risk and market risk is key for the question at hand: specific risk, in the terms of insurance actuaries, is "poolable"; market risk is not, because by definition the variables which are the source of market risk are common, in greater or lesser degree, to most or all companies. The independence assumption critical to the successful application of the law of large numbers is absent. Highly

diversified portfolios of common stocks, for example, do not tend toward risklessness; indeed, the degree of market risk remaining in a perfectly diversified portfolio can be quite substantial.

In lay terms: although occasionally a company will go bankrupt for reasons relative to specific risk, there is a substantial likelihood that the Guarantee Corporation will find that in times of broad economic distress, large numbers of sponsoring companies for which it has assumed pension obligations will go bankrupt almost simultaneously. Pension liabilities are already on the order of several hundred billion dollars. It is not inconceivable that the Guarantee Corporation could find itself owing enormous amounts—say, tens of billions—to pension beneficiaries of bankrupt companies.

These requirements can be disregarded if the risk to be insured is modest in relation to the resources of the insurer. For example, the federal government issues flood insurance even though entire areas can be wiped out by floods and the very existence of federal flood insurance encourages development of land exposed to such floods. The key, however, is the dollar magnitude of the risk. Unfortunately, the risk to be insured in the case of pension claims dwarfs that in the case of flood damage.

The PBGC's role under ERISA is often likened to that of the FDIC. Without liability insurance, the comparison is a valid one. With it, the comparison is severely misleading. The first line of defense for the FDIC is a bank's equity, for the FDIC can move in on a troubled bank and seize its assets while they still exceed its liabilities.[1] To assure timely action, the FDIC has a standard reporting format and a task force of examiners to keep it informed on the condition of member banks. In contrast, liability insurance deprives the PBGC of its first line of defense: the power to reach employer assets.

Is ERISA ex post facto law? If the liability insurance provision were expunged from ERISA, with the consequent legal implication that pension claims are claims on corporate assets per se, would it be construed as an ex post facto law? A number of business spokesmen, constitutional lawyers, and members of Congress contend that ERISA creates corporate liabilities that were not contemplated when

---

[1] The merger of Security National Bank into the Chemical Bank and Trust Company provides an example. The FDIC stepped into the situation when Security National's equity appeared inadequate. A merger subsequently occurred without penalty to the bank's depositors or the FDIC.

the great majority of pension plans were established. They contend that in doing so, ERISA has retroactively altered private contracts to the benefit of one group of persons (pension participants) and to the detriment of another group (company shareholders and creditors); and that this is tantamount to impairing the integrity of contracts and confiscating property without due process of law. Such acts, they argue, are explicitly prohibited by the Fourteenth and Fifteenth Amendments to the U.S. Constitution.

Whereas the courts have been zealous in protecting the integrity of contracts and in assuring due legal process in matters involving property rights, they have also been intent upon "piercing the corporate veil" to assure that corporations act in good faith.

Consider the following example: "A" has a history of making promises to "B" that were not legally binding; later a law is passed to force "A" to honor these promises. Should that law be invalidated or abrogated on the ground that "A" would be unfairly burdened since the promises would never have been made had A expected to have to honor them?

Let "A" be an employer and "B" a pension claimant. "A" has promised "B" certain pension benefits under certain qualifying conditions but neglected to provide funding adequate to fulfill the promises. In addition, "A" has taken risks with pension assets in hope of investment gains from which only A would have profited. Does ERISA violate the integrity of the pension contract in requiring that a company make good on its pension promises?

ERISA can be regarded as confiscatory only if companies had no intention of honoring their pension promises to employees. If they did intend to pay the benefits promised, ERISA's liability provisions impose no undue penalty; these provisions merely compel the honoring of promises made by plan sponsors and accepted by plan participants.

CONCLUSION

With the advent of ERISA, the pension game has suddenly turned serious. Yet the act, as we have noted, is by turns ambiguous and self-contradictory. The ambiguities and contradictions will be worked out in the courts and in changes in the law. As one prominent pension actuary said, "Now that we have the act, the next step is to work out a philosophy under which it can be administered."

Unfortunately, the working out will come too late for employers who have to make decisions with far-reaching, irreversible consequences today—decisions relating to the level of pension compensation, to the risk policy in the pension portfolio, and so on.

In this book, we have attempted to provide concerned parties who are unwilling—if not, indeed, unable—to wait for clarifying legislation with a glimpse of that philosophy.

The old question, "Will the employee get his or her benefits?" is replaced by a new question: "Who will bear the burden?" In the stead of the individual pension beneficiary, the pension act has placed a new government agency with enormous powers—the Pension Benefit Guaranty Corporation. As we have noted, the Guaranty Corporation has the power to reach beyond the assets in a company pension fund to the assets of the sponsoring company itself.

But, the Guaranty Corporation's power is effectively frustrated, if, in the absence of willing private insurors, it is obliged to "insure" the employer company against its own claims on company assets. The Guaranty Corporation is then left in the position of assuming an unconditional pension liability in return for a conditional claim against the employer. This is an awkward—indeed, a dangerous—position for the Guaranty Corporation.

If the Guaranty Corporation should falter, then, of course, the U.S. government—which is to say, the U.S. taxpayers—can step in. But there is no way to provide something for nothing. If the pension beneficiary is to get the full value of his or her benefits, somebody must pay for those benefits. If the sponsoring companies cannot pay for the benefits—possibly by requiring of strong companies that they bear some of the burden of the weak—then the taxpayer will have to pick up the difference.

It is our conviction that basic principles of finance will determine the final form of our pension legislation and its interpretation. To the extent that those principles have been flouted in the original architecture of the act, the act will be corrected because the pension system has become too important to be permitted to fail.

Failure of the private pension system would be viewed by voters as a failure of private enterprise—as a breach of faith by the corporations who accepted the burden of pension obligations in return for the fruits of labor for which they would otherwise have been required to pay current wages. Then too, the private pension system, with its enormous and still growing assets, represents the last, best chance to give the bulk of American voters an important personal stake in capitalism.

This does not mean that we despair for the future of ERISA; quite the contrary. We have argued that, with discreet pruning, ERISA can become the act its authors meant it to be.

Appendixes

Appendix A

Legal evolution of pension claims

Paralleling the quantitative growth of the U.S. private pension system has been a qualitative change in the claims created by that system.

From its beginnings in colonial times until the time of the Great Depression, pension planning, where it existed at all, was entirely within the employers' prerogative. Their liability was nil. Whether or not to have a pension plan; who was to be eligible for participation and when; at what rate claims to benefits were to be vested; what benefits were to be paid; whether or not to fund the plan, and how; whether, when, and how to modify the plan, or just discontinue it— all of these decisions were wholly the business of owners and managers, not that of governments nor, with very few exceptions, that of unions. Typical was the disclaimer in an early pension plan: "This pension plan is a voluntary act on the part of the Company and is not to be deemed or construed . . . as giving any employee an enforceable right against the Company. The Board of Directors of the Company reserves the right to alter, amend, annul or cancel the plan or any part of it at any time."[1] The first major adjudication affecting pension rights,[2] decided by the U.S. Supreme Court in 1889, denied the plaintiff any right *to his or her own contribution* to a corporate pension fund on the ground that since the contribution was not voluntary, it conferred no property right, and therefore no valid

---

[1] Quoted by Ralph Nader and Kate Blackwell, *You and Your Pension* (New York: Grossman Publishers, 1973).

[2] Cited by Paul S. Harbrecht, *Pension Funds and Economic Power* (New York: Twentieth Century Fund, 1959).

claim predicated on such right. At most, the employer had a *moral* obligation to pay pension benefits that the employer had voluntarily committed to pay—not a legally enforceable liability for payment. As recently as 1957, in *Kravitz* v. *Twentieth Century-Fox Film Corporation,* a New York court ruled that a pension plan was a gratuitous promise—one for which the employees gave no consideration, and hence unenforceable—continued employment for a long period not being regarded by the court as "sufficient consideration."[3]

By that time, however, the evolution of the legal status of pension claims had moved a step further. To ameliorate the harsh consequences of the gratuity doctrine, a few courts began in the 1930s to have recourse to the doctrine (in equity law) of "promissory estoppel" which, in general terms, states that "a promise which the promisor should reasonably expect to induce action or forebearance is binding if injustice can be avoided only by enforcement of the promise." Through application of this doctrine, the promises implicit in formulation of a pension plan were treated as having a certain binding character, from which the promisor could not arbitrarily free himself or herself.

World War II marked another turning point in the legal status of pension claims. The courts began to recognize that pension plans concerned not only the employer but the employee and the retiree. In the *Inland Steel* case of 1947, a U.S. Circuit Court ruled that pensions were a form of remuneration, and therefore properly subject to collective bargaining. Since collective bargaining usually resulted in a contract, the status of pension claims fell under the protection of the law of contracts. This protection was later extended to what were called "unilateral contracts." The legal doctrine of such contracts (authoritatively enunciated in the 1950s) held that a pension plan, even if voluntary and not entered into or maintained under union compulsion, constitutes an offer by an employer to enter into a unilateral contract to provide benefits under specified conditions, which offer is implicitly accepted by employees who remain in the service of the employer, thus fulfilling the conditions of the plan. Whether pension plans derived from collective bargaining and were accordingly bilateral contracts—which is the case today of the majority of plans, especially those with the largest number of

---

[3] A case cited in Dan M. McGill, *Fulfilling Pension Obligations,* published for the Pension Research Council, University of Pennsylvania by Richard D. Irwin, Inc., 1962.

participants—or were construed as unilateral contracts, they had the legal status of contracts and, as such, were enforceable at law.

But the pension rights so recognized were enforceable only against the pension fund itself, not against the employer who had set up the fund. As Max Block, a prominent actuary, commented: "Our colleagues in the legal profession have by now made sure that the standard pension plan includes two things: *a very explicit limitation of total terminating liabilities to the amount of pension fund assets* and a more or less complex set of priorities to be applied if the assets fall short of the total actuarial value of immediate and deferred retirement benefits."[4]

Actually, things aren't quite as neat as Mr. Block makes them appear. Even before ERISA, companies were still obligated to pay vested benefits as long as they were able (which meant short of bankruptcy), when the pension funds accumulated proved inadequate. Indeed, some experts argued that pension participants' claims extended beyond corporate income and included corporate assets. However, they had no right to force companies into bankruptcy in order to make good their claim on corporate assets before the assets were dissipated. And in the event of bankruptcy, pension claims were junior to all others. For both these reasons, claims against corporate income and assets remained empty.

In a relatively small number of cases, largely confined to the steel and petroleum industries, pension claims against corporate income and assets had more substance. The way the pension plans were written pledged the corporation's own resources to the satisfaction of pension claims. The funds accumulated by the plans were merely convenient conduits into which corporate contributions could be poured at one end and pension benefits paid at the other. They had the legal and financial status of corporate reserves that in no way limited the liability of the corporation itself.

But such plans were a tiny minority of the 120,000 or so defined-benefit plans that were in force before the enactment of ERISA. In all these cases, the termination of a plan—because of business failure, liquidation, merger or reorganization, change in location or ownership, or whatever other reason, whether a purely arbitrary act or one compelled by business necessity—meant that pension

---

[4] In the *Proceedings,* 1973–1974, of the Conference of Actuaries on Public Practice, vol. 22. [Italics added.]

claims vested under it were satisfied only to the extent of adequacy of plan funds. That is why so many pension participants remained exposed to the risks taken with pension assets, and why so many pension claims remained unsatisfied.

Appendix **B**

Major provisions of ERISA

PLANS COVERED

The act applies in varying degrees to almost every type of employee benefit plan maintained by any company, of whatever size, in any way involved in interstate commerce. The main exceptions are governmental plans, church plans, and plans primarily for the benefit of nonresident aliens. ERISA applies with particular stringency to defined-benefit retirement plans, that is those plans which are intended to provide stated pension benefits upon retirement. The law does not require the establishment of a pension plan, nor does it prohibit modification or termination of plans, but it does establish minimum standards for existing and future plans.

ELIGIBILITY FOR PARTICIPATION

No employee older than 25 years and with more than one year of service with a company, or hired more than five years before normal retirement age, may be excluded from participation in that company's pension plan. A year of service is defined as 1,000 or more hours of service in a 12-month period (either calendar or fiscal year).

VESTING

All pension plans must guarantee future retirement benefits to participants who complete a specified number of years of service, even if employment terminates before the employee reaches normal retirement age.

Plans must choose one of the three following vesting schedules:

1. Ten-year vesting: 100 percent vesting after ten years of service.
2. Graded vesting: 25 percent vesting after five years of service, then increasing by 5 percent per year to 50 percent vesting after ten years of service; thereafter increasing by 10 percent a year to 100 percent vesting five years later.
3. Rule of 45: 50 percent vesting when a participant's age and years of service add up to 45; then increasing by 10 percent a year to 100 percent vesting five years later.

All employee contributions to a pension fund, and investment returns on such contributions, are fully vested from the beginning.

ERISA restricts the "break-in-service" rules that tended in the past to nullify or limit vesting in most pension plans. Once an employee has achieved any degree of vesting, his or her rights may not be impaired by any break of service. However, before vesting, an employee may lose credit for benefits already accumulated if there occurs a year's break in service, which is defined as fewer than 500 hours of employment during that year. If a break does not occur before an employee has vested claims, the employee can still resume progress towards vesting if the break is less than the period of prior service.

The law imposes application of one of three alternative rules designed to restrict differentiation of the rates at which pension benefits accrue during different periods of employment. Under the first rule, the accrual rate for any given year cannot be more than one third greater than that for any other year. Under the second rule, the minimum rate of benefit accrual before the end of $33\frac{1}{3}$ years of participation in a plan is 3 percent of the maximum benefit to which a participant would be entitled were the participant to remain in the company's employ for 40 years before retirement. Under the third rule, a participant's accrued benefit at any given date must be a specified portion of the benefit to which the participant would be entitled at normal retirement age.

Vested benefits are not to be voided even upon a participant's death. At his or her option, benefits will continue to be paid to the deceased's spouse (though the amount of benefit may be scaled down as actuarially determined). Nor are vested benefits forfeitable because an ex-employee joins a competing company, does something else that a pension-sponsoring company may find offensive, or is convicted of a crime.

FUNDING

Normal costs of a company's pension plans—that is, the costs attributable to benefit claims deriving from employee services in a given year—must be fully funded that year.

Liabilities deriving from employees' past services must be amortized over a period not to exceed 40 years and, for new plans or for increased liabilities of old plans because of liberalization of benefits, over a 30-year period. "Experience" gains and losses—that is, those deriving from the difference between purchase and market prices of pension assets and from over- or underfunding (as when wage increases are greater or less than the actuary had anticipated) —will have to be actuarially determined at least once every three years; and such gains or losses must be amortized over a 15-year period from the time of determination.

Pension assets must now be valued on the basis of a "reasonable actuarial method of valuation that takes into account fair market value."

The actuarial assumptions and procedures on the basis of which pension liabilities are calculated will have to be certified as "reasonable" by an actuary acceptable to the Treasury and Labor Departments; and the annual reports on the financial condition of pension plans will have to be signed by certified public accountants.

Companies that fail to meet minimum funding standards will be subject to a 5 percent nondeductible penalty tax, and if they do not correct the funding deficiency within 90 days after notification by the IRS, they will be subject to additional nondeductible penalty taxes equal to 100 percent of the funding deficiency.

However, a company may obtain an extension of up to ten years to satisfy the minimum funding requirements if it cannot meet them without causing business hardships that could adversely affect the interests of plan participants. Employers may also obtain waivers under such circumstances in up to 5 out of 15 consecutive plan years, and the amounts waived may be amortized in up to 15 years.

The maximum tax-deductible employer contribution for any year may not exceed normal costs for that year plus the amount required to fund initial unfunded past service liability over a ten-year period.

FIDUCIARY RESPONSIBILITY

ERISA mandates "fiduciary responsibility" for any pension plan trustee, for investment managers of pension assets, and for any other persons who may have responsibility and authority in the management of a plan or in controlling, allocating, and disposing of the plan's assets. Fiduciaries, so defined, must discharge their duties solely in the interests of the participants in given plans. They are made liable for asset losses resulting from violation of the "prudent man" rule, which requires them "to discharge their duties with the care, skill, prudence and diligence which a prudent man acting in a like capacity would use under conditions prevailing at the time." More specifically, a fiduciary is prohibited from such transactions as dealing with the plan for his or her own account or selling anything to, buying anything from, receiving a gift from, or lending money from plan assets to, a "party-in-interest" under a plan (i.e., the plan-sponsoring employer, plan participants, the unions involved, or persons providing services to the plan) or investing more than 10 percent of plan assets in the employer's securities or real property (present investments over 10 percent must be divested by 1984).

The act requires diversification of the investments of the plan, geographically, by industry and by type of vehicle, so that the risk of loss be minimized, except when selling off fund assets in order to diversify would itself result in substantial loss and would clearly not be prudent at the time.

ERISA empowers participants and beneficiaries—or their unions, or the U.S. Department of Labor acting on their behalf—to sue fiduciaries for "fiduciary irresponsibility" on such charges as pursuing inappropriate investment policies or making imprudent investment decisions, or persuading professional investment managers, placed in charge of some part of plan assets, to do either. A fiduciary may also be held liable for losses caused by other fiduciaries if the fiduciary concealed their acts or was negligent in not seriously trying to stop their breach of responsibility.

ERISA specifically voids provisions in pension plans or in trust agreements that relieve fiduciaries of personal liability for losses resulting from their acts or from their failure to act appropriately.

REPORTING AND DISCLOSURE

Every pension plan to which ERISA applies must file with the Department of Labor annually:

1. An audit of the plan, made and signed by a CPA.
2. An actuarial valuation of the pension plan made by an actuary acceptable to the Departments of Treasury and Labor.
3. An itemized listing of all pension assets, with their maturity dates, maturity values, interest or dividend rates, purchases cost, and market value at time of filing.
4. A report of every transaction involving a "party-at-interest" or more than 3 percent of the fund's assets.

Participants in every plan covered by ERISA must be given:

1. A plan booklet—to be revised at least once every five years—which includes a comprehensive plan description and a summary description of the plan "written in a manner calculated to be understood by the average plan participant." Every new participant in a plan must be given the booklet within 90 days of participation.
2. Summaries of any material changes in a plan.
3. Summaries of annual reports filed with the Department of Labor.
4. At participants' request, copies of the full annual report, all contracts and instruments of the plan, any union agreement relating to the plan, as well as statements of accrued credits towards vesting and vested benefits.
5. For persons terminating employment, a statement of accrued vested benefits.

PLAN TERMINATION INSURANCE

ERISA created The Pension Benefit Guaranty Corporation within the Department of Labor, with the Secretaries of Labor, Commerce, and the Treasury as directors, to insure pension benefits in the event a plan terminates without sufficient funds to meet vested obligations.

The insured benefit is limited to $750 per month (but not more than 100 percent of the employee's average earnings during his or her highest paid period). This amount will be automatically increased in step with increases in the social security wage base. The guarantee does not extend to liberalization of benefit formulas granted during the five years prior to plan termination.

During the first two years after enactment of ERISA, the insurance premium was fixed at $1 per year per participant for single-employer plans and $0.50 per participant in multiemployer plans. In succeeding years the premium may be adjusted according to a variety of options available to the Guaranty Corporation and to pension-sponsoring companies.

A pension plan may be terminated voluntarily (with certain restrictions) or involuntarily by the Guaranty Corporation, upon court order. The corporation may bring action in court to terminate a plan if the plan (1) fails to meet the minimum funding standards, (2) is unable to pay benefits when due, (3) is administered improperly, or (4) if the liability of the Guaranty Corporation for fulfilling claims deriving from the plan is likely to increase unreasonably.

Should a plan be terminated, whether voluntarily or involuntarily, the Guaranty Corporation would assume primary responsibility for meeting all guaranteed pension claims under the plan. It will discharge this responsibility using first the funds accumulated by the plan. Should the funds prove inadequate, the pension-sponsoring company will be liable for 100 percent of the underfunding, but in no case may this liability exceed 30 percent of the company's net worth. To make sure that corporate assets are not dissipated or otherwise made unavailable to discharge pension liabilities, the Guaranty Corporation is empowered to place a lien on the company's property (and, in the case of an unincorporated business, on the employer's personal property). This lien would have the same priority as a federal tax lien, and would therefore be senior to unsecured liabilities (except wages due).

However, no later than September 1977, the Guaranty Corporation will have to provide insurance against such "contingent liability." All pension-sponsoring companies may be required to purchase such insurance coverage either from qualified private insurance carriers or from the Guaranty Corporation or both. The protection offered by this insurance will not be available until 60 months of premiums have been paid. However, premiums may be paid retroactively for some part of the 60-month waiting period. This could make the protection available before the end of the decade.

Appendix C

Actuarial cost methods

As we noted in Chapter 2, there are a variety of actuarial cost methods for funding a pension plan. All have the same objective—the accumulation of a fund that will be adequate to pay pension benefits to plan participants who retire. The actuarial cost methods differ chiefly in the timing of annual pension contributions.

The five recognized funding methods fall into one of two broad categories—accrued benefit methods and projected benefit methods. Under an accrued benefit cost method, the annual pension expense reflects the benefits that accrue during the current year. By contrast, under a projected benefit method, the pension expense reflects a portion of the benefits that are expected to be earned over the entire working lives of the plan participants.

The principal accrued method (i.e., the unit credit method) and two of the projected methods (i.e., the entry age normal and the attained age normal methods) involve liabilities for unfunded past-service costs. When a plan is adopted and one of those funding methods is used, the portion of pension costs assigned to past years is called the "past-service cost" or "supplemental liability," while the portion assigned to each subsequent year is called the "normal cost." If the plan is later amended to reflect improved benefits, the portion of costs assigned to past years is called "prior service costs." Unfunded past or prior service costs are generally amortized over periods of 10 to 40 years. By contrast, if the individual level premium or the aggregate methods are used, past-service costs are not identified separately but are projected for the working lives of the plan participants, are amortized as such, and included as part of the annual normal costs.

A 1973 study by the Conference Board revealed that the entry age normal method was the most popular of the leading actuarial cost methods and was used by 43 percent of the companies surveyed.[1] Next in order of popularity was the unit credit method (used by 20 percent of the companies), followed by the aggregate method (17 percent), and the attained age normal method (6 percent), and "other" methods (14 percent). Briefly, the methods differ in the following respects.

The entry age normal method is a projected benefit method under which contributions are made from the date the individual entered the plan to the date of the actuarial valuation. The contributions are made in level annual amounts, or sometimes as a level percentage of payroll. While the method is supposed to be applied on an individual basis, in practice it is often applied on an aggregate basis for all covered employees, with benefits funded over their remaining work lives. For years other than the initial year of the plan, there may be a past-service cost or frozen supplemental liability, which must be amortized according to the provisions of ERISA. As a funding method, the entry age normal method is popular with companies that have trusteed plans or use deposit administration contracts.

The unit credit method is the best known of the accrued benefit cost methods, under which pension benefits are funded as the employee puts in his or her service and earns them. As a result, normal costs include the benefits earned by the employee for that particular year, while unfunded past-service costs are amortized over a period of 10 to 40 years. The unit credit label derives from the fact that the benefits unit is usually a fixed amount of money per year of service or a fixed percent of the employee's earnings per year of service. Because older workers generally have more years of service and higher earnings, the normal costs under the unit credit method tend to increase as the work force and the plan population mature. Companies that fund through group annuity contracts almost always use the unit credit method, but it can also be used in trusteed plans.

The aggregate method is a projected benefit cost method that is applied on a collective basis to include all plan participants as a group. Unfunded past-service costs are not identified separately but

---

[1] The Conference Board, *Financial Management of Company Pension Plans* (New York, 1973) p. 25.

are included as part of the normal costs, which are spread over the remaining working lives of plan participants. Contributions are usually computed as a percentage of payroll.

The individual level premium method is similar to the aggregate method, only it is applied on an individual rather than on a collective basis. Initial costs are high under both methods because past-service costs, which are not separately identified, are amortized over the remaining working lives of the plan participants. For a plan with older workers, this results in a short amortization period and, consequently, a high level of initial contributions. However, normal costs under the individual level premium method, which are usually computed as a percent of payroll, ultimately drop to the level of the entry age normal method.

The attained age normal method is a modification of the aggregate or the individual level premium methods, with the unfunded past-service costs determined under the unit credit method and amortized over a period of 10 to 40 years, in accordance with the provisions of ERISA. Normal-service costs are usually determined on a percentage of payroll basis, but they do not decline as sharply as under the aggregate or the individual level premium methods. The latter method is generally used in conjunction with individual insurance or annuity policies, whereas the aggregate and the attained age normal methods are generally used with trusteed plans.

The actuarial cost methods can be modified in several ways, and they differ in their treatment of actuarial gains and losses. Suffice to say, actuaries try to tailor the method to the needs, work force, financial position, and expected future of the plan sponsor. For a more detailed discussion of funding methods, consult the following:

References

Allen, Everett, Jr., Melone, Joseph J., and Rosenbloom, Jerry S. *Pension Planning: Pensions, Profit Sharing, and Other Deferred Compensation Plans.* 3d ed. Homewood, Ill.: Richard D. Irwin, Inc., 1976.

American Institute of Certified Public Accountants. "Accounting for the Cost of Pension Plans," *Accounting Principles Board Opinion No. 8.* New York, November 1966.

Berin, Barnet N. *Pensions: A Guide to the Technical Side.* Chicago: Charles D. Spencer & Associates, Inc., 1973.

Financial Accounting Standards Board. "An Analysis of Issues Related to Accounting and Reporting for Employee Benefit Plans." Stamford, Conn., October 1975.

Financial Executives Research Foundation. *Financial Aspects of Private Pension Plans.* New York, 1975.

McGill, Dan M. *Fundamentals of Private Pensions.* 3d ed. Homewood, Ill.: Richard D. Irwin, Inc., 1975.

Marples, William F. *Actuarial Aspects of Pension Security.* Homewood, Ill.: Richard D. Irwin, Inc., 1965.

Melone, Joseph J. and Allen, Everett, Jr. *Pension Planning.* Homewood, Illinois: Richard D. Irwin, Inc., 1972.

The Conference Board. *Financial Management of Company Pension Plans.* New York, 1973.

Appendix D

Pension costs and unfunded liabilities—A survey of 40 major corporations

In Chapters 2 and 3, we presented summary statistics on the pension costs and unfunded liabilities of a sample of major American corporations. The study encompassed the four largest companies, on the basis of total employment, in ten major industries. The 1973 pension figures of the 40 companies were disclosed in a special report written by one of your authors, *Pension Costs and Unfunded Liabilities,* published by Merrill Lynch, Pierce, Fenner & Smith, Inc., in October 1974. In the following pages, the 1970–73 pension expense growth rate figures are from that report. The other figures are as of year-end 1974, unless otherwise noted, and are based on a May 1975 presentation by two of the authors, "Valuing Corporations with Pension Liabilities," before the Institute for Quantitative Research in Finance.

We must again caution that the pension expense and liability figures of the various companies are not really comparable, due to different funding methods, actuarial assumptions, eligibility standards, and vesting provisions. Nevertheless, the sample offers useful aggregate data on the size and growth of pension costs and unfunded liabilities.

The pension expense and liability figures listed in the following pages were determined by the companies and their actuaries and were disclosed in the annual and 10-K reports they filed with the Securities and Exchange Commission. Unless we have noted otherwise, the pension fund asset figures are valued at market rather than cost. If the company did not disclose the data in annual or 10-K reports, we relied upon the figures published in *Money Market Directory 1976*. The *Directory* is compiled during the August–October period of the preceding year and is based on questionnaires mailed to major corporations and financial institutions. Thus, the 1976 *Directory* offered market valuations of pension fund assets as of the latest valuation date in mid-1975, which for most companies was year-end 1974.

Automobile industry

	General Motors	Ford	Chrysler	American Motors
Total assets of pension fund (million)..	$ 4,326	$ 2,391	$ 1,031	$ 123
Number of employees...............	734,000	464,731	255,929	33,143
1974 pension expense (millions)...... $	819	$ 385	$ 256	$ 24.8
As a percent of funds available.....	33%	40%	213%	37%
As a percent of pretax profits.......	49%	66%	def.	59%
Per employee.................... $	1,115	$ 829	$ 1,002	$ 747
Unfunded vested benefits (millions)... $	3,400	$ 1,465	$ 1,201	$ 80
As a percent of pension assets......	79%	61%	116%	65%
As a percent of net worth.........	27%	23%	45%	21%
Per employee.................... $	4,632	$ 3,152	$ 4,693	$ 2,414
Total unfunded pension liability (millions).................... $	6,100	$ 2,700	$ 1,821	$ 190
As a percent of pension assets......	141%	113%	177%	154%
As a percent of net worth.........	49%	43%	68%	50%
Amortization period.............	30 yr.	30 yr.	30 yr.	40 yr.
Capital structure (adjusted for UVB)..	100%	100%	100%	100%
Unfunded vested benefits..........	25%	19%	22%	17%
Long-term debt.................	7%	19%	27%	17%
Stockholders' equity.............	68%	62%	51%	66%
Annual growth of pension expense:				
1974.........................	+14%	+15%	+28%	+18%
1973.........................	+12%	+ 8%	+12%	+19%
1972.........................	+ 9%	+30%	+18%	+ 7%
1971.........................	+78%	+49%	+25%	+ 7%
1970.........................	− 0%	+ 2%	+ 6%	+44%

Note: American Motors is on a September 30th fiscal year. *Money Market Directory 1976* was the source of pension fund asset data for American Motors. Pension fund assets of the other companies were at book value, as disclosed in annual reports. Chrysler's adjusted capital structure assumes a UVB limited to 30 percent of net worth.

Chemical industry

	DuPont	Union Carbide	Monsanto	Dow
Total assets of pension fund (millions)...	$ 2,011	$ 750	$ 396	$ 350
Number of employees.................	136,866	109,566	60,926	53,300
1974 pension expense (millions)........	$ 150	$ 87.2	$ 47.2	$ 65.4
As a percent of funds available.......	18%	9%	8%	6%
As a percent of pretax profits........	22%	10%	8%	6%
Per employee.....................	$ 1,097	$ 796	$ 775	$ 1,227
Unfunded vested benefits (millions).....	None	$ 60	$ 68.1	160
As a percent of pension assets.......	—	8%	17%	46%
As a percent of net worth..........	—	2%	4%	8%
Per employee.....................	—	$ 548	$ 1,118	$ 3,002
Total unfunded pension liability (millions)......................	$ 413	$ 450	$ 132	n.a.
As a percent of pension assets........	21%	60%	33%	n.a.
As a percent of net worth..........	11%	18%	8%	n.a.
Amortization period...............	20 yr.	40 yr.	15–30 yr.	n.a.
Capital structure (adjusted for UVB)....	100%	100%	100%	100%
Unfunded vested benefits............	0%	2%	3%	5%
Long-term debt...................	17%	26%	25%	40%
Stockholders' equity...............	83%	72%	72%	55%
Annual growth of pension expense:				
1974............................	+48%	+36%	+31%	+120%
1973............................	− 6%	+39%	+ 0%	+ 19%
1972............................	+12%	+ 3%	− 1%	+ 21%
1971............................	+ 2%	+12%	+14%	+ 20%
1970............................	−16%	+ 0%	+ 6%	+ 15%

Note: *Money Market Directory 1976* was the source of pension fund asset data for all but DuPont. DuPont's pension fund assets were at book value, as disclosed in the annual report.

n.a.—not available.

Drug industry

	Warner Lambert	Johnson & Johnson	Am. Home Products	Charles Pfizer
Total assets of pension fund (millions).....	$ 65	$ 152	n.a.	$ 100
Number of employees..................	58,500	54,300	$45,703	39,500
1974 pension expense (millions)..........	$ 24.1	$ 15.7	$ 13.6	$ 15.7
As a percent of funds available.........	8%	5%	3%	7%
As a percent of pretax profits..........	9%	6%	3%	7%
Per employee........................	$ 411	$ 289	$ 297	$ 397
Unfunded vested benefits (millions).......	None	None	None	None
As a percent of pension assets..........	—	—	—	—
As a percent of net worth.............	—	—	—	—
Per employee........................	—	—	—	—
Total unfunded pension liability (millions).	$ 78.4	n.a.	None	$ 24
As a percent of pension assets..........	121%	n.a.	—	24%
As a percent of net worth.............	8%	n.a.	—	3%
Amortization period..................	13–40 yr.	10 yr.	—	40 yr.
Capital structure (adjusted for UVB)......	100%	100%	100%	100%
Unfunded vested benefits..............	0%	0%	0%	0%
Long-term debt......................	10%	3%	0%	23%
Stockholders' equity..................	90%	97%	100%	77%
Annual growth of pension expense:				
1974.............................	+17%	+18%	−19%	+34%
1973.............................	+24%	+15%	+30%	+ 7%
1972.............................	+ 8%	+19%	− 9%	+15%
1971.............................	+34%	+10%	+ 9%	+42%
1970.............................	+20%	+17%	+ 4%	+49%

Note: American Home Products reports its pension expense after taxes. As a result, we had to estimate the before-tax expense on the assumption of a 48 percent tax rate. *Money Market Directory 1976* was the source of pension fund asset data.

n.a.—not available.

Electrical equipment industry

	General Electric	Westinghouse	Combustion Engineering	Babcock & Wilcox
Total assets of pension fund (millions)..	$ 2,762	$ 877	n.a.	$ 151
Number of employees................	404,000	199,248	40,765	40,075
1974 pension expense (millions).......	$ 168	$ 75.2	$ 16.7	$ 26.3
As a percent of funds available......	14%	27%	18%	31%
As a percent of pretax profits.......	17%	36%	23%	45%
Per employee.....................	$ 415	$ 377	$ 409	$ 655
Unfunded vested benefits (millions)....	$ 345	$ 444	$ n.a.	$ 98.9
As a percent of pension assets.......	12%	51%	n.a.	65%
As a percent of net worth..........	9%	23%	n.a.	29%
Per employee.....................	854	2,228	n.a.	2,468
Total unfunded pension liability (millions)......................	$ 458	$ 587	$ 65.8	$ 124
As a percent of pension assets.......	17%	67%	n.a.	82%
As a percent of net worth..........	12%	31%	19%	36%
Amortization period...............	20 yr.	30 yr.	30 yr.	40 yr.
Capital structure (adjusted for UVB)...	100%	100%	100%	100%
Unfunded vested benefits...........	7%	16%	n.a.	17%
Long-term debt...................	24%	30%	23%	42%
Stockholders' equity...............	69%	54%	77%	41%
Annual growth of pension expense:				
1974...........................	+24%	+25%	+19%	+15%
1973...........................	+26%	+24%	+21%	+13%
1972...........................	+12%	+13%	+12%	+45%
1971...........................	+37%	+36%	+22%	+23%
1970...........................	+26%	+57%	+18%	+35%

Note: *Money Market Directory 1976* was the source of pension fund asset data for Babcock & Wilcox. Pension fund assets of General Electric and Westinghouse were at book value, as disclosed in annual reports.

n.a.—not available.

Food processing industry

	Beatrice Foods	Kraftco	General Foods	Borden
Total assets of pension fund (millions).....	n.a.	$ 200	$ 295	$ 118
Number of employees...................	64,000	50,410	48,000	46,700
1974 pension expense (millions).......... $	20.0	$ 22.9	$ 26.2	$ 13.3
As a percent of funds available.........	7%	11%	10%	8%
As a percent of pretax profits..........	8%	13%	11%	8%
Per employee....................... $	312	$ 454	$ 545	$ 285
Unfunded vested benefits (millions)....... $	7.8	$ 16.8	None	$ 31.0
As a percent of pension assets..........	n.a.	8%	—	26%
As a percent of net worth.............	1%	2%	—	4%
Per employee....................... $	122	$ 333	—	$ 664
Total unfunded pension liability (millions).	n.a.	$ 60.2	n.a.	$ 80.1
As a percent of pension assets..........	n.a.	30%	n.a.	68%
As a percent of net worth.............	n.a.	7%	n.a.	10%
Amortization period.................	30 yr.	40 yr.	Interest only	30 yr.
Capital structure (adjusted for UVB)......	100%	100%	100%	100%
Unfunded vested benefits..............	1%	2%	0%	3%
Long-term debt.....................	24%	22%	22%	29%
Stockholders' equity.................	75%	76%	78%	68%
Annual growth of pension expense:				
1974.............................	+14%	+16%	+39%	+21%
1973.............................	+41%	+ 1%	− 8%	+34%
1972.............................	+38%	+ 8%	− 1%	+ 2%
1971.............................	+14%	+ 9%	+30%	+ 5%
1970.............................	− 9%	+ 6%	+87%	−33%

Note: The fiscal year for Beatrice Foods ends on February 28th of the following year, and General Foods is on a March 31st fiscal year. Pension fund assets of General Foods were at market value, as disclosed in the annual report. *Money Market Directory 1976* was the source of pension fund asset data for Kraftco and Borden.

n.a.—not available.

Miscellaneous

	Caterpillar Tractor	Eastman Kodak	Lockheed	Western Union
Total assets of pension fund (millions)...	$ 575	$ 955	$ 625	$ 72
Number of employees.................	76,993	124,100	62,100	15,045
1974 pension expense (millions)........	$ 88.6	$ 271	$ 100	$ 32.4
As a percent of funds available.......	20%	19%	74%	49%
As a percent of pretax profits........	24%	24%	287%	98%
Per employee.....................	$ 1,151	$ 2,187	$ 1,610	$ 2,154
Unfunded vested benefits (millions).....	$ 350	$ 130	$ 420	$ 233
As a percent of pension assets........	61%	14%	67%	324%
As a percent of net worth...........	24%	4%	1,585%	40%
Per employee.....................	$ 4,546	$ 1,048	$ 6,763	$15,487
Total unfunded pension liability (millions)......................	880	n.a.	n.a.	$ 291
As a percent of pension assets........	153%	n.a.	n.a.	404%
As a percent of net worth...........	60%	n.a.	n.a.	50%
Amortization period................	30 yr.	30 yr.	30 yr.	40 yr.
Capital structure (adjusted for UVB)....	100%	100%	100%	100%
Unfunded vested benefits...........	17%	4%	49%	19%
Long-term debt...................	31%	2%	51%	54%
Stockholders' equity...............	52%	94%	0%	27%
Annual growth of pension expense:				
1974............................	+44%	+ 9%	+27%	+ 8%
1973............................	+ 9%	+15%	− 1%	+ 8%
1972............................	+22%	+ 5%	+ 5%	− 4%
1971............................	+40%	− 2%	+17%	+ 7%
1970............................	+ 8%	+ 2%	+11%	+20%

Note: *Money Market Directory 1976* was the source of pension fund asset data for Caterpillar Tractor and Western Union. Pension assets of Kodak and Lockheed were at market, as disclosed in annual reports. Pension expense figures for Kodak include profit sharing contributions for the years 1972–74. Pension expense figures for Western Union include amounts charged to plant and equipment.

   n.a.—not available.

Office equipment industry

	IBM	Sperry Rand	Honeywell	Xerox
Total assets of pension fund (millions)...	$ 1,530	$ 662	$ 200	$ 254
Number of employees.................	292,350	92,963	92,173	101,380
1974 pension expense (millions)........	$ 334	$ 54.8	$ 41.5	$ 97.4
As a percent of funds available.......	9%	18%	25%	11%
As a percent of pretax profits........	10%	23%	34%	13%
Per employee......................	$ 1,142	$ 589	$ 450	$ 961
Unfunded vested benefits (millions).....	$ 190	None	$ 34	$ None
As a percent of pension assets........	12%	—	28%	—
As a percent of net worth...........	2%	—	4%	—
Per employee......................	$ 650	—	$ 369	—
Total unfunded pension liability (millions).....................	368	n.a.	$ 131	None
As a percent of pension assets.......	24%	n.a.	66%	—
As a percent of net worth..........	4%	n.a.	14%	—
Amortization period...............	10–25 yr.	10 yr.	30 yr.	—
Capital structure (adjusted for UVB)....	100%	100%	100%	100%
Unfunded vested benefits...........	2%	0%	2%	0%
Long-term debt...................	3%	30%	32%	37%
Stockholders' equity...............	95%	70%	66%	63%
Annual growth of pension expense:				
1974...........................	+29%	+18%	+42%	+ 6%
1973...........................	+17%	+37%	+ 3%	+14%
1972...........................	+30%	+ 0%	+21%	+33%
1971...........................	+28%	+36%	− 5%	+14%
1970...........................	+23%	− 2%	+27%	+28%

Note: Sperry Rand's fiscal year ends on March 31st of the following year. *Money Market Directory 1976* was the source of pension fund asset data on all four companies. The $254 million asset figure refers to the market value of Xerox's profit sharing trust. The figures for Xerox include the company's contribution to its profit sharing plan and some minor pension plans.

n.a.—not available.

Retail industry

	Sears	Penney	Kresge	Woolworth
Total assets of pension fund (millions)	$ 2,201	$ 351	n.a.	$ 144
Number of employees	339,800	193,000	134,000	100,000
1974 pension expense (millions)	$ 111	$ 30.0	$ 11.5	$ 13.7
As a percent of funds available	15%	12%	6%	12%
As a percent of pretax profits	18%	14%	6%	14%
Per employee	$ 326	$ 155	$ 86	$ 137
Unfunded vested benefits (millions)	$ 115	None	None	$ 50.7
As a percent of pension assets	5%	—	—	35%
As a percent of net worth	2%	—	—	5%
Per employee	$ 338	—	—	$ 507
Total unfunded pension liability (millions)	$ 48.7	$ 38.8	$ 13.0	$ 15.1
As a percent of pension assets	2%	11%	n.a.	10%
As a percent of net worth	1%	3%	1%	2%
Amortization period	40 yr.	30 yr.	n.a.	10–40 yr.
Capital structure (adjusted for UVB)	100%	100%	100%	100%
Unfunded vested benefits	2%	0%	0%	4%
Long-term debt	17%	21%	17%	30%
Stockholders' equity	81%	79%	83%	66%
Annual growth of pension expense:				
1974	−20%	− 9%	+33%	+13%
1973	+10%	+ 6%	+28%	+12%
1972	+11%	+33%	+27%	+ 1%
1971	+20%	+20%	+14%	+ 4%
1970	− 2%	− 2%	+ 9%	+ 6%

Note: The pension expense figures for Sears and Penney include profit sharing as well as pension contributions. Data on Sears relates to Sears alone and does not include the pension assets, pension and profit sharing expense, profits and employees of Allstate or other unconsolidated subsidiaries. Pension fund assets of Sears include the profit sharing fund but exclude the supplemental pension plan. Asset data on Penney is for the total retirement plan and pretax profits include Penney Financial but exclude other unconsolidated subsidiaries. Kresge's pretax profits do not include the insurance subsidiary. Pension asset data on Woolworth was taken from *Money Market Directory 1976* and pretax profits exclude F. W. Woolworth & Co., Ltd. For all of the firms, the fiscal year ends on January 31st of the following year.

n.a.—not available.

Steel industry

	U.S. Steel	Bethlehem Steel	Armco Steel	Republic Steel
Total assets of pension fund (millions).....	$ 2,399	$ 732	$ 408	$ 428
Number of employees...................	187,503	122,000	52,121	44,230
1974 pension expense (millions)..........	$ 170	$ 154	$ 54.8	$ 55.0
As a percent of funds available.........	14%	20%	13%	16%
As a percent of pretax profits..........	16%	25%	15%	18%
Per employee........................	$ 907	$ 1,261	$ 1,052	$ 1,243
Unfunded vested benefits (millions).......	$ 400	$ 1,029	$ 177	$ 422
As a percent of pension assets..........	17%	141%	43%	99%
As a percent of net worth.............	9%	41%	14%	34%
Per employee........................	$ 2,133	$ 8,434	$ 3,400	$ 9,541
Total unfunded pension liability (millions).	1,600	$ 1,169	$ 243	$ 447
As a percent of pension assets..........	67%	160%	60%	104%
As a percent of net worth.............	36%	47%	19%	36%
Amortization period..................	n.a.	30 yr.	n.a.	n.a.
Capital structure (adjusted for UVB)......	100%	100%	100%	100%
Unfunded vested benefits.............	7%	24%	11%	25%
Long-term debt......................	23%	21%	20%	18%
Stockholders' equity.................	70%	55%	69%	58%
Annual growth of pension expense:				
1974.............................	+89%	+33%	+18%	+ 8%
1973.............................	+22%	+43%	+38%	+21%
1972.............................	+18%	+43%	+33%	+26%
1971.............................	−41%	+21%	+ 1%	+ 3%
1970.............................	+44%	+15%	+15%	+24%

Note: *Money Market Directory 1976* was the source of pension asset data for Armco Steel. Pension assets of the other companies were at book value, as disclosed in annual reports. The adjusted capital structures of Bethlehem and Republic assume a UVB limited to 30 percent of net worth.

n.a.—not available.

Tire and rubber industry

	Goodyear	Firestone	Uniroyal	Goodrich
Total assets of pension fund (millions)..	$ 580	$ 510	$ 158	$ 290
Number of employees................	154,166	120,000	63,845	48,929
1974 pension expense (millions).......	$ 79.3	$ 51.0	$ 64.2	$ 39.7
As a percent of funds available......	21%	16%	44%	30%
As a percent of pretax profits.......	26%	19%	78%	44%
Per employee.....................	$ 514	$ 425	$ 1,006	$ 810
Unfunded vested benefits (millions)....	$ 331	$ 119	$ 492	$ 155
As a percent of pension assets.......	57%	23%	311%	53%
As a percent of net worth..........	19%	8%	78%	22%
Per employee....................	$ 2,147	$ 989	$ 7,706	$ 3,166
Total unfunded pension liability (millions).....................	429	$ 387	$ 525	$ 321
As a percent of pension assets......	74%	76%	332%	111%
As a percent of net worth..........	25%	27%	83%	45%
Amortization period..............	25 yr.	25 yr.	30 yr.	30 yr.
Capital structure (adjusted for UVB)...	100%	100%	100%	100%
Unfunded vested benefits..........	12%	6%	17%	13%
Long-term debt..................	35%	30%	44%	40%
Stockholders' equity..............	53%	64%	39%	47%
Annual growth of pension expense				
1974..........................	+34%	+28%	+20%	+10%
1973..........................	+ 3%	+10%	+12%	+46%
1972..........................	+ 3%	− 2%	+ 6%	+ 8%
1971..........................	+14%	+11%	+10%	+37%
1970..........................	+ 6%	+12%	+22%	− 1%

Note: Firestone is on an October 31st fiscal year. *Money Market Directory 1976* was the source of pension fund asset data for all companies except Firestone. Firestone's pension fund assets were at book value, as disclosed in the annual report. Uniroyal's adjusted capital structure assumes a UVB limited to 30 percent of net worth.

Appendix E

How to use option theory to compute the value of pension claims

I. The following description of the Black-Scholes option formula in this section of Appendix E is adapted from "The Pricing of Options and Corporation Liabilities" by Fischer Black and Myron Scholes, *Journal of Business,* January 1973.

The greater the value of the underlying asset, the less the value of the put option. When the asset value is much less than the exercise value, the option is almost sure to be exercised. The current value of the option will then be approximately equal to the value of a pure discount bond that matures on the same date as the option, with a face value equal to the striking price of the put.

If the expiration date of the option is very far in the future, then the value of a bond that pays the exercise price on the maturity date will be very low and the value of the put option will approach zero.

If the expiration date is very near, the value of the option will be approximately equal to the exercise value minus the asset value, or zero, if the asset value is greater than the exercise price. Normally, the value of an option declines as its maturity date approaches, if the value of the asset does not change.

The value of the option cannot be worth more than the exercise price. On the other hand, its value cannot be negative and cannot be less than the exercise value minus the asset value. In order to derive the formula for the value of options, Black and Scholes make a number of idealizing assumptions, including:

a. The short-term interest rate is known and is constant through time.

b. The value of the asset follows a random walk in continuous time with a variance rate proportional to the square of its price. Thus the distribution of possible asset values at the end of any finite interval is log normal. The variance rate of the return on the stock is constant.

c. The asset pays no dividends or other distributions.

d. The option can only be exercised at maturity.

e. Transaction costs are ignored.

Under these assumptions, the value of the option will depend only on the value of the asset and time and on variables that are taken to be known constants. Let x be the asset value, t the current date, σ^2 the variance rate of the return on the asset, ln the natural logarithm, and N the cumulative normal density function.

Writing t^* for the maturity date of the option and c for the exercise value, we know that:

$$w(x, t^*) = c - x, \; xc$$
$$= 0, \; xc$$

There is only one formula $w \; (x, t)$ that satisfies the differential equation subject to the boundary condition. This formula must be the valuation formula for the (European) put option.

This formula is:

$$w(x, t) = x[N(d_1) - 1] - c[e^{r(t-t^*)}N(d_2) - 1]$$
$$d_1 = \frac{\ln x/c + (r + \frac{1}{2}\sigma^2)(t^* - t)}{\sigma\sqrt{t^* - t}}$$
$$d_2 + \frac{\ln x/c + (r - \frac{1}{2}\sigma^2)(t^* - t)}{\sigma\sqrt{t^* - t}}$$

The net value of the corresponding pension claim is:

$$c[e^{r(t-t^*)}N(d_2)] + x[1 - N(d_1)]$$

with all variables defined as before.

A table of the function N appears as Table 1.

The partial derivative of the value of the put option with respect to the value of the underlying asset is:

$$w_1(x, t) = N(d_1) - 1$$

where $N(d_1)$ is defined as above.

TABLE 1

The normal distribution*

d_1 or d_2	$\mathcal{N}(d)$
0.0	0.500 000
0.1	0.539 828
0.2	0.579 260
0.3	0.617 911
0.4	0.655 422
0.5	0.691 462
0.6	0.725 747
0.7	0.758 036
0.8	0.788 145
0.9	0.815 940
1.0	0.841 345
1.1	0.864 334
1.2	0.884 930
1.3	0.903 200
1.4	0.919 243
1.5	0.933 193
1.6	0.945 201
1.7	0.955 435
1.8	0.964 070
1.9	0.971 283
2.0	0.977 250
2.1	0.982 136
2.2	0.986 097
2.3	0.989 276
2.4	0.991 802
2.5	0.993 790
2.6	0.995 339
2.7	0.996 533
2.8	0.997 445
2.9	0.998 134
3.0	0.998 650
3.1	0.999 032
3.2	0.999 313
3.3	0.999 517
3.4	0.999 663
3.5	0.999 767
3.6	0.999 841
3.7	0.999 892
3.8	0.999 928
3.9	0.999 952
4.0	0.999 968
4.1	0.999 979
4.2	0.999 987
4.3	0.999 991
4.4	0.999 995
4.5	0.999 997

* William Feller, *Probability Theory and Its Applications* (New York: John Wiley & Sons, Inc.), 1950.

II.   Calculation of the net value of a pension claim will appear formidable at first glance, involving as it does three equations and numerous independent variables, the values of which must be supplied. But, of these variables, only one or two—the discount rate r and the variance rate v—will pose any problems. This section describes simple ways to get satisfactory approximations for these variables.

If the pension obligation is more nearly a real obligation expressed in current dollars than a nominal obligation, then the entire calculation can most conveniently be carried through in real terms. Whatever happens to nominal interest rates, the best assumption about what the real interest will be over any but the shortest horizon is—as noted in the text—3 percent.

The variance rate is only slightly harder to determine. If time is expressed in years, the variance rate, like the interest rate, should be expressed as a rate *per year*. It is useful to view the variance as the sum of four elements:

1. The market risk in the employer's corporate assets. Unless the employer's own corporate debt is of very low quality, the variance in the employer's equity will approximate the desired number.
2. The specific risk in the employer's corporate assets.
3. The market risk in the pension assets.
4. The specific risk in the pension assets. If the pension portfolio is reasonably well diversified, this element may be ignored.

Letting:

x_e = market value of employer's corporate net worth,
x_p = market value of the pension fund,
σ_m^2 = variance rate for market as a whole,
B_e = market sensitivity of the employer's common stock,
B_p = market sensitivity of the pension portfolio (allowing for any debt securities in the portfolio),
σ_e^2 = residual variance for the employer's common stock,
σ_p^2 = residual variance for the pension portfolio (if this element is not being ignored),

we have the following formula for the overall variance rate employed in the calculation of the value of the pension claim:

$$\frac{(x_e D_e + x_p B_p)^2 \sigma_m^2 + x_e^2 \sigma_e^2 + x_p^2 \sigma_p^2}{(x_e + x_p)^2}$$

As we have noted, there are potentially four sources of investment risk contributing to the overall variance. Of these four, two are perfectly correlated—the market risk in the employer's assets and the market risk in the pension assets. The combined exposure to the market risk is the sum of the market sensitivities ("betas"), weighted by the value of the respective assets.

The specific risk in the employer's assets is defined statistically independent of the market risk, as is the specific risk in the pension portfolio. Unless the pension portfolio is invested in the securities of the employer company (an unlikely event under ERISA), the two sources of specific risk are also likely to be reasonably independent of each other. It is a well-known theorem in statistics that if two random variables are statistically independent, the variance of the sum is the sum of the variances. In the present instance there are three such random variables—the market risk in the employer's assets, the specific risk in the employer's assets, and the specific risk in the pension assets. The total variance is therefore the sum of the variances contributed by these three sources of risk.

The coefficient of each of the three terms in the numerator of the formula is weighted by a coefficient equal to the aggregate value of the assets exposed to that particular source of risk, squared. The reader can readily satisfy himself or herself that if the variance of one share of the particular common stock is σ^2, the variance of the portfolio containing two shares of that common stock is $4\sigma^2$, the variance of the portfolio containing ten shares of the common stock is $100\sigma^2$, and so forth.

The sum in the numerator is the absolute variance of the combined employer and pension assets. What is desired, however, is not the absolute variance but rather the variance per dollar invested. Since the dollar weightings in the numerator are all squared, the variance per dollar invested can be derived from the absolute variance only by dividing the latter by the square of the dollars invested—which is to say, by the square of the sum of the employer's assets and pension assets—hence the denominator in the formula. This formula is strictly correct only if, as noted, corporate claims against the employer are of high quality when assessed on a conventional basis and if the specific risks in the corporation and the pension fund are uncorrelated (i.e., statistically independent).

If, as recommended, the computation of the value of the pension claim is carried through in real rather than nominal terms, then, strictly speaking, the elements in the formula for the variance rate should be supplied in real rather than nominal terms. Since year-to-year uncertainly about the price level one year ahead is typically small, however, the use of nominal quantities in this formula will understate the variance rate in real terms only slightly.

III.   To demonstrate the use of these techniques in estimating the value of a pension claim, we pose the following simplified problem: J. Jones is an employee of Electronic Dynamics, a small but rapidly growing technology based company. Currently 29 years old, Jones expects to retire at age 65. The company's pension fund, invested entirely in common stocks, is already as large as the net worth of the company itself, measured at market value. The pension fund is perfectly diversified but, of course, the company is not. It has been determined that the firm has a beta of 0.8 and a residual variance of 0.0171.

Electronic Dynamics, contemplating rapid growth for the foreseeable future, pays no dividend. Despite Jones's tender age, Jones is the company's oldest employee. Because Jones is Electronic Dynamics' oldest employee, Jones's pension claim will be senior to the pension claim of all other employees. Therefore the latter's claim can be ignored in calculating the value of Jones's claim. It may seem unlikely that a company could grow rapidly for 36 years (the time remaining until Jones retires), let alone that it can go 36 years without paying dividends. For simplicity, however, assume that its present dividend policy will continue. Ignoring the possibility that Jones will leave the company before Jones's pension rights are fully vested, what is J. Jones's claim to a lump-sum payment at age 65 really worth?

The first task is to compute the variance rate appropriate to the assets underlying Jones's pension claim. Using the facts given we make the following substitutions in the formula for the variance rate: $x_b = 0.5$, $x_p = 0.5$, $beta_b = 0.8$, $beta_p = 1.0$, $\sigma_e^2 = 0.0171$. Finally we assume that the variance rate σ_m^2 for the market as a whole is 0.0225 (corresponding to the standard deviation on the change in market level over one year of 15 percent). Substituting these values in the formula we find that the overall variance rate for the assets underlying Jones's claim is just equal to that of the market as a whole—0.0225 per year.

The value of Jones's claim depends on the relation between its

TABLE 2

(1)	(2)	(3)	(4)	(5)	(6)	(7)	(8)	(9) Net value
x/c	d_1	$N(d_1)$	$1 - N(d_1)$	$x/c[1 - N(d_1)]$	d_2	$N(d_2)$	$e^r(t - t^*)N(d_2)$	c
0.5	0.878	0.771	0.229	0.114	0.18	0.429	0.145	0.259
1.0	1.648	0.951	0.049	0.049	0.752	0.774	0.264	0.313
1.5	2.1	0.982	0.018	0.027	1.20	0.885	0.301	0.328
3.0	2.87	1.000	0	0	1.97	0.975	0.332	0.332

* Column (9) is the net value of the pension claim divided by the face value. In this example, this number is column (5) plus column (8).

aggregate value and the true current value of the underlying assets. To demonstrate the way in which fluctuations in the value of the underlying assets affect the value of Jones's claim, we shall carry out the computations for several assumed values of this ratio. Table 2 displays the details of the computations, the results of which are displayed graphically in Figure 1.

FIGURE 1

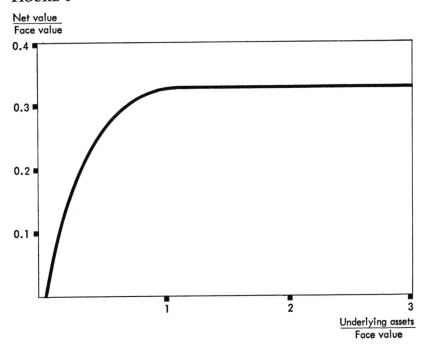

The reader will recall that the Black-Scholes option model consists of three equations. Accordingly, the calculation of the net value of the claim breaks down into three parts:

1.   The calculation of the function of d_1,
2.   The calculation of d_2, and
3.   The calculation of the overall expression for the net value of the pension claim which depends on these two functions.

To calculate the values for d_1 and d_2 the reader needs the natural logarithm of the ratio x/c, the square root of the time to maturity (i.e., the time until the pension claim falls due), which in the J. Jones example is $\sqrt{36}$, or 6, and the total variance rate, which for the example we have estimated at 0.0225 per year. The reader will also need v—the square root of the variance rate—which as we already know is 0.15, and the riskless rate of interest, which we assume to be 0.03. When one substitutes these values into the equations of d_1 and d_2, the values shown in columns (2) and (6) of Table 2 are obtained.

The next step is to substitute these values into the cumulative normal distribution function (see Table 1). Because the normal distribution is strictly symmetrical, the value of $N(d)$ can be calculated for negative values of d from Table 1 in the following way: Observe by how much the value of $N(d)$ exceeds 0.5 for the positive value of d corresponding to the negative value for which the value of $N(d)$ is desired. Subtract that difference from 0.5. The result is the value of $N(d)$ corresponding to the negative value of d. Picking values off Table 1 in this fashion, we obtain the numbers displayed in columns (3) and (7) of Table 2.

Column (5) results from multiplying the contents of column (4) by column 1. The only complexity in calculating column (8) from column (7) is the calculation of the expression $e^r (t - t^*)$. This is, of course, the present value of one dollar, discounted at the rate r for $(t - t^*)$ years. Accordingly it can be approximated, despite the discrete compounding employed, by simply referring to conventional interest tables, but it can be estimated more exactly by using tables of natural logarithms.

Column (9) is, of course, the sum of the figures in columns (5) and (8). It shows the present value of J. Jones's pension claim, per dollar of *face* value. The calculation is made for four different ratios of the value of the underlying assets to the face value of the pension claim. The table shows among other things that when the face value of this pension claim is covered three times by the current value of the underlying assets, the present face value of this claim is nearly as large as the value discounted at the riskless rate (0.34).

IV. What is a stream of pension plans worth? How does one evaluate a stream of pension claims?

In general, of course, each will have a different value and its own associated pension put. Consider a particular claim in the midst of such a stream. It gets paid in full before subsequent claims get anything. On the other hand, claims prior in time will be paid in full before it gets anything. It follows that in relation to the assets available to meet them, pension claims rank in seniority in the order in which they fall due.

The problem is that the Black-Scholes solution as presented in their published papers does not fit the case of a stream of pension claims precisely (to be sure, it was not designed for this purpose). Consider, for example, the last two pension claims in a stream. As a function of the value of the underlying assets, the value of the last claim will be known when the next to last is paid; and since the value of the sum is also known, all are a function of the underlying assets.

Question: Given this function, can the value of the two claims at some still earlier time be derived? Answer: No, not exactly, because of the two claims being added together one (the one still to be paid) is subjected to a put and the other (the one to be paid currently) is not. The function describing the combined value is not one that arises (at any time, to any factor of proportionality) in the course of a standard Black-Scholes solution.

The problem is not with the partial differential equation that is the heart of their approach. The partial differential equation described in their paper applies to any stream of pension claims. The problem is rather that the boundary condition for the conventional option problem (the kinked payoff curve), which fits the single pension claim, rarely if ever applies in the case of a stream of claims.

The solution to these problems is, of course, to solve the Black-Scholes partial differential equation for the boundary conditions specific to a stream of pension claims. We shall not undertake that formidable task here. Instead we shall offer two crude and highly approximative ways to applying the *standard* Black-Scholes solution to the problem of a stream of claims. Although they will fail to give the exact answer for the reasons noted, taken together they will bracket the exact answer.

1. The lower limit

Since claims prior in time will be paid in full before the claim at issue gets anything, they stand in relation to that claim precisely like creditors' claims on the employer corporation. One crude way to allow for these claims in reckoning the net value of the claims at issue, therefore, is to subtract their present value (discounted at the riskless rate) from the "underlying assets."

But what about the variance rate? The assumption so far (arbitrary, to be sure) has been that the (relative) variance rates for (1) the employer's net worth, and (2) the pension assets, are constant over time and over fluctuations in the value of these assets. Subtracting pension claims from these assets has the effect of changing the assumption about variance rates, because it is now the original assets *less the prior pension claims* (which we shall call the "adjusted assets") that have the constant relative variance rate (which we shall call the "adjusted variance rate"). Compute the present value discounted at the riskless rate of all prior claims, subtract it from the current value of the underlying assets, compute an adjusted variance rate on the assets net of prior claims, using the formula at the end of this appendix, and apply the formula for the value of the net pension claim using the adjusted asset figure for the underlying assets ("adjusted x") and the adjusted variance rate figure for the variance rate (s^2).

The resulting estimate of the net value of the claim in question will be low for the following reasons: (*a*) It assumes that adjusted assets bear the entire risk (variance) associated with underlying assets whereas the prior pension claims, being risky, bear some of the variance. (*b*) Like the employer's equity, the pension claim enjoys a put option against prior pension claims. This method of estimation ignores the contribution of the put to the value of the claim in question. (*c*) As noted, the Black-Scholes model assumes a constant variance rate. Applying the model in this way implicitly assumes that the variance rate of the adjusted assets, rather than the original underlying assets, is constant.

2. The upper limit

The second way—adding the value of the prior claims to the pension claim at issue—leaves the variance rate assumption regarding the original assets unchanged but assumes that the prior claims, as well as the claim at issue, are at risk, and that the current claim shares *pro rata* with the prior claims in that risk. Compute the present value of all claims prior to the claim in question, discounted at the riskless rate. Appreciate that present value forward to the time at which the claim in question falls due, again at the riskless rate. Add the value of the prior claims calculated this way to the face value of the current claim. Substitute this combined value for the face value of claim (*c*). Allocate to the claim in question its *pro rata* share of the combined net value given by the formula.

This method exaggerates the value of the claim in question for the following reasons: (*a*) It permits the claim in question to share *pro rata* with claims that in fact have absolute priority over the current claim, and will get paid in full before the current claim gets anything. (*b*) This method implicitly assumes that prior claims are exposed to the risk in the underlying assets for longer than they really are, diminishing the importance of their combined claim on the underlying assets.

The attached work sheet is designed to streamline the computation of the upper and lower estimates of the net value of each claim in a stream of pension claims. To use it, start at the top and work down, filling out each row completely before going on to the next.

Fill in the face value of the individual claims across the top, together with the time at which they occur. In addition to this information, the work sheet requires the current value of the underlying assets, *x*, and the variance rate associated with those asset σ^2.

The first step in the computation is to calculate the time that will elapse until each of the claims fall due (row 2). The second is to use those times to transform the face values of individual claims (row 3) into gross present values, discounting at the riskless rate (row 4). The third is to cumulate these present values, working from the left-hand side of the work sheet (row 5). The fourth is to subtract the running cumulative sum of these values from the current value of the underlying assets, obtaining what we call the "adjusted *x*" (row 6). The final step in this part of the computation is the so-called "adjusted variance" (row 7).

It can be estimated as follows:

Let y be the present value of prior claims. Then we have:

$$s^2 = \frac{x^2}{(x - y)^2} \sigma^2$$

where, as before, σ^2 and x are respectively the variance rate and current value of the original assets.

At this point we have all the data required to apply the formula for the net value of a pension claim. Note, however, that in calculating the net value of a given claim we use the adjusted figure (x) and adjusted variance (s^2) computed for the previous column. In other words: Since, in applying the formula this way, the face value of a claim enters explicitly into the computation of its net present value, it would be double counting to use an adjusted asset value or variance rate in that computation that already allowed for the claim.

The procedure for calculating the upper limit on the individual pension claims follows a somewhat different pattern. In order to obtain the "face value" equivalent of these claims, refer back to row 5 of the work sheet ("cumulative present value") and appreciate those numbers forward to the time at which each claim falls due, again at the riskless rate of interest. Because of the way the numbers in row 5 were computed, in each case these "face value equivalents" (row 9) will include the face value of the claim falling due. Using the unadjusted asset figure (x) and the unadjusted variance (σ^2), substitute this number for c in the formula to obtain an estimate of the net value of the combined claims (row 10).

Now compute for each claim the ratio of its face value to the "effective face value" of the combined claims (row 11). This ratio is the basis for allocating the estimated net value of the combined claims between that claim and all prior claims. Apply this ratio to the estimate of the net value of the combined claims (row 10) to obtain the upper estimate of the value of the claim (row 12). Repeat these steps for each claim in the stream.

If one adds up the low estimates of the net present values of all the pension claims in the stream, and subtracts them from the current value of the underlying assets, the economic value of the employer's equity will of course be overestimated. Similarly, if one adds up the upper-limit estimates of the net present values of the claims in a stream and subtracts them from the current value of the underlying assets, the economic value of the employer's equity will be underestimated. Indeed, there is nothing in principle to prevent the latter estimate from being negative.

Worksheet for calculating upper and lower estimates of the net value of pension claims

Time of payment	t_0	t_1	t_2	$\cdots$	t_n
Time until payment	0	$t_1 - t_0$	$t_2 - t_0$		$t_n - t_0$
Face value of claim		c_1	c_2		c_n
Gross present value					
Cumulative present value					
"Adjusted x"					
s^2 ("adjusted σ^2")					
$w_{\text{low}}(x, t)$					
Cumulative present value appreciated to t					
$w_{\text{cum}}(x, t)$					
c_t/cum PV					
$w_{\text{high}}(x, t)$					

V. In this presentation we have suppressed an important additional complexity. If this pension plan terminates, the employee is likely to get paid less than if the plan continues until his claim falls due. There are at least three reasons for this:

1. As noted, in many pension plans benefit payments are based on the current dollar level of the employee's salary in his last five

years of employment. If the pension plan terminates before the employee retires, he is deprived of the upward adjustments in current dollar terms in his pension benefits that would result from raises in current dollar terms between termination of the plan and his scheduled retirement.

2. When the full pension liability is computed on an actuarial basis, it allows for the fact that if the plan continues, many currently unvested employees will continue with the plan long enough to become vested. On the other hand, if the plan terminates, unvested employees are deprived of the opportunity to vest.

3. Benefit increases are often written into labor contracts which, under the Pension Act, will become guaranteed by the PBGC only over a period of time. If the plan terminates before such increases are guaranteed, the PBGC has no obligation to make good on them.

The combined effect of these three considerations can be substantial. The result is, of course, that the Guarantee Corporation's obligation is substantially less if the employer company terminates than if it does not. The question immediately arises: Is the employer free to terminate voluntarily in order to reduce his pension obligation from the higher number to the lower one? Under the Act, the employer must have the Guarantee Corporation's permission to terminate—permission the Guarantee Corporation can deny unless the employer can demonstrate a "legitimate business purpose" for termination. Since termination is likely to be very expensive for the Guarantee Corporation, the only "legitimate business purpose" it is likely to recognize is insolvency (presumably in the sense of the augmented balance sheet). To this extent therefore, the employee, like the Guarantee Corporation, is counting on the continued solvency of the pension plan to bail him out. It follows that the employer's "pension put" is actually divided between the Guarantee Corporation and the employee with the put against the Guarantee Corporation based on the termination rather than the full value of the employee's pension claim.

Appendix F

Development of the pension multiplier[1]

In exploring the relationship between the riskiness of the old equity and the riskiness of the new equity, we are interested in that portion of investment risk that is directly additive across diverse kinds of companies. It follows that the relevant source of risk for our purposes is what is called "market" risk—the sensitivity of the asset in question to fluctuations in the general stock market. In the calculations that follow, we shall represent the level of the stock market by m.

With these symbols in mind we are ready to write an expression of the riskiness of the new equity. Before doing so, however, we note that when we refer to an asset as risky we are referring not to absolute sensitivity of the asset in question to market fluctuations but rather to its relative sensitivity—in other words, to the percentage change in the value of the asset in question induced by a unit change in the level of the general stock market. The change in the value of the new equity induced by such a change in the level of the general market is $\frac{de'}{dm}$, and the percentage change is $\frac{1}{e'}\frac{de'}{dm}$. In terms of our expression for e' we can obtain $\frac{de'}{em}$ by differentiation.

Whereas both the old equity and the new pension assets are in general sensitive to market fluctuations, the pension liability, by assumption, is not, hence its derivative with respect to m is zero. From these considerations we arrive at Equation (1):

---

[1] To be read in conjunction with pages 77–80.

$$\frac{1}{e'}\frac{de'}{dm} = \frac{\dfrac{de}{dm} + \dfrac{da}{dm}}{e + a - l} \tag{1}$$

It is immediately apparent from Equation (1) that the new equity is always riskier than the old equity, even if pension assets are entirely invested in Treasury Bills and $\dfrac{da}{dm}$ equals zero. We know this intuitively for so long as the pension assets a are less than the present value of the pension liability l (so long as the plan is not fully funded), we have added leverage to the company. In this case, the denominator will always be less than e. The numerator of the fraction in Equation (1) will always be greater than or equal to $\dfrac{de}{dm}$. Thus $\dfrac{1}{e'}\dfrac{de'}{dm}$ will always be equal to or greater than $\dfrac{1}{e}\dfrac{de}{dm}$.

$$\frac{1}{e'}\frac{de'}{dm} > \frac{1}{e}\frac{de}{dm} \tag{2}$$

Our main purpose is to explore the relation between the riskiness of the new equity and the riskiness of the old equity. This relation is defined by the following equation:

$$\frac{1}{e'}\frac{de'}{dm} = \frac{\dfrac{de}{dm} + a\dfrac{1}{c'}\dfrac{de'}{dm}}{e + a - l} \tag{3}$$

Equation (3) represents the simplest case—that is, the case in which companies' pension assets are invested entirely in the (new) equities of other companies with comparable pension plans. The numerator of the large fraction in the right-hand member of Equation (3) is the absolute risk—that is to say, the absolute sensitivity of the augmented corporate assets to market fluctuations. If the pension portfolio is vested entirely in equities of corporations with similar pension situations, then a times $\dfrac{1}{e'}\dfrac{de'}{dm}$ is the (absolute) contribution of the pension portfolio to the market risk in the augmented assets. On the other hand, $\dfrac{de}{dm}$ is the contribution of the absolute market risk in the old equity, by definition. The total absolute risk in e' is of course the sum of the two contributions. The denominator in the right-hand member is simply the expression for e'; division by this amount converts absolute risk to relative risk. Transposing and solving for $\dfrac{1}{e'}\dfrac{de'}{dm}$ we get Equation (4), which expresses the relation between the relative risk in the old equity and the relative risk in the new equity:

$$\frac{1}{e'}\frac{de'}{dm} = \frac{1}{e-l}\frac{de}{dm} = \frac{1}{1-l/e}\frac{1}{e}\frac{de}{dm}, \qquad (4)$$

from which it follows that the pension multiplier is

$$\frac{1}{1-l/e}.$$

To demonstrate the use of the pension multiplier concept we offer the following example: 20 companies most widely held in portfolios managed by large banks[1] constitute upwards of 50 percent of the equity portfolios of these banks (see Table F–1).

TABLE F–1

Fraction of equity assets of large trust banks invested in 20 largest holdings (year-end 1974)

Morgan Guaranty Trust	46%
Bankers Trust	41
Chase Manhattan	50
Citibank	51

According to the 1975 SEC survey, the average pension fund devoted 44 percent of the pension assets under management to debt securities. These 20 companies have pension assets amounting to $21.7 billion at the end of 1974. The market value of their equity conventionally reckoned was $153.1 billion. They had unfunded vested benefits of roughly $7.3 billion.

From these facts we deduce that of the $21.7 billion in pension assets held by these banks for the 20 companies in question, 9.5 billion was in debt securities and most of the remainder, 12.2 billion, was in equities. Applying the information from Table F–1 that the 20 largest holdings constitute roughly 50 percent of equity

---

[2] As described in Chapter 7.

holdings of such trust companies, we estimate that $6.1 billion of the pension money managed by these banks for the 20 most widely held companies was invested in the shares of these same companies, and roughly $6.1 billion in the shares of other companies.

This problem demonstrates both of the complexities anticipated in our discussion of the pension multiplier: On one hand, not all the pension assets of the companies in question are held in equity securities and on the other, not all the equity securities held are shares in the 20 companies. The first problem is remedied by offsetting against the pension liability of these companies the holdings in their pension portfolios of debt securities. We estimate the total pension liability by adding to the unfunded vested benefits ($7.3 billion) the total pension assets ($21.7 billion) obtaining for our estimate $29.0 billion. We subtract from the total liability the value of the debt securities in the 20 companies' security portfolios ($9.5 billion), obtaining for the "effective liability" $19.5 billion.

Because pension assets invested in the shares of companies without pension plans are not subject to the vicious circle that leads to the pension multiplier, they add to the conventional rather than the augmented equity. Accordingly we add $6.1 billion to the market value of the 20 companies' conventional equity ($153.1 billion) obtaining $159.2 billion—the "effective conventional equity."

We substitute the effective liability for *"l"* and the effective conventional equity for *"e"* in the formula for the pension multiplier obtaining 1.14. Under the assumptions in this example, the augmented equity of the 20 most widely held corporations contains on average 14 percent more systematic or market risk than their conventional equity.

Offered here merely to demonstrate the mechanics of the computation, this number seriously understates the true value of the pension multiplier for the following reasons: (1) The unfunded vested benefit understates the pension liability because it ignores those unfunded past-service costs that will become vested in the future. (2) As the sample companies included in the calculation expand from the 20 largest holdings to the several hundred companies found in pension portfolios, the average quality of the pension plans included in the sample will decline sharply. (3) The larger the sample considered the larger will be the fraction of the equity holdings of the pension plans in the sample that are invested in shares of the same companies. (For example, if the sample included all publicly held companies this ratio would rise to 100 percent.) (4) Half the equity assets are assumed to be invested in securities representing companies with no pension funds.

Thus the real multiplier is much higher than this model calculation suggests—perhaps as high as 30 to 50 percent.

Appendix G

Glossary of terms

Actuarial assumptions: The assumptions—about such matters as mortality rates among employees and pensioners of a pension-sponsoring organization, turnover rates among employees, rates of wage inflation, and investment return on pension fund assets—used by actuaries in reckoning the cost of, and accordingly the required annual contributions to, a particular pension plan. (See **Mortality rate, Turnover rate, Investment return,** and **Pension cost.**)

Actuarial cost methods: The particular formulas and techniques used by actuaries to determine the amounts and incidence of annual contributions required for adequate funding of particular pension plans. (See **Funded benefits.**)

Actuarial gains (losses): Also called **Experience gains (losses).** The effect on actuarially calculated annual contributions of (1) deviations between actual prior experience (with respect to mortality, turnover, investment return, etc.) and the actuarial assumptions employed; or of (2) changes in actuarial assumptions.

Actuarial valuation: The process by which an actuary estimates the present value of benefits to be paid under a given pension plan and, on that basis, calculates the amounts of annual contributions or of accounting charges. (See **Present value.**)

Claimant: A person, whether employed or retired, with claims, recognized as valid by his or her employer or by law, to specific benefits under some pension plan.

Contributory plan: A pension plan under which the employees covered contribute some stipulated part of the funding of the benefits they are to receive.

Defined benefit plan: See **Pension plan.**

Funded benefits: That portion of the total benefits, including those not yet vested, estimated as having to be paid under a pension plan that is, as of a given date, covered by funds already accumulated for future payment of benefits.

Funded vested benefits: That portion of total vested benefits covered by accumulated funds. (See **Vested benefit.**)

Insured plan: A pension plan under which benefits are to be paid by a particular insurance company on the basis of an insurance contract between that company and a pension-sponsoring employer.

Investment return: The combination of yield (interest, dividends, rents, royalties, and other income) and capital gains (or losses) resulting from investing and trading a pension fund's assets. (See **Pension assets.**)

Mortality rate: Death rate—the proportion of the number of deaths in a specified group to the number living at the beginning of the period in which the deaths occur. Actuaries use mortality tables, which discriminate death rates by age and sex, and sometimes also by occupation or other characteristics. The mortality tables currently being used differ very widely.

Normal cost: That portion of the annual contribution assigned, under the actuarial cost method used, to liabilities for benefit payments derived from years of employment subsequent to inception of a pension plan. (See **Past-service cost.**)

Option: The right (acquired at an option cost) to buy, and call for delivery (a call), or sell, and make delivery (a put) of specified securities, or other property, at specified prices within specified times (the periods designated in each option contract). (See **Pension put.**)

Participant: Any person covered by a pension plan, both those still employed and those already retired and receiving pension benefits.

Past-service (or prior-service) cost: That portion of the annual contribution assigned, under the actuarial method used, to liabilities for benefit payments attributable to years of employment prior to the inception of a pension plan. (See **Normal cost.**)

Pension assets: The securities and other property purchased with cash contributions to a pension fund, and with investment returns on the fund, and presumably available—upon sale at prevailing market price and so converted into cash—for payment of pension benefits as they fall due.

Pension Benefit Guaranty Corporation: Also designated PBGC, the Guaranty Corporation, or the Corporation. A U.S. government agency, set up under ERISA within the Department of Labor, with a board of directors consisting of the Secretaries of Labor, Commerce, and the

Treasury, intended to insure that participants in pension plans covered by ERISA will receive all benefit payments to which they are entitled under their respective plans, within certain limits defined by ERISA. The Guarantee Corporation is empowered by the act to collect premiums and attach the corporate assets of pension-sponsoring companies in order to be able to pay benefits under terminated plans.

Pension costs: The sum of a pension-sponsoring company's annual contributions to a pension fund over the life of the plan being funded. For noncontributory plans, the ultimate cost equals the total benefits paid plus the expenses incurred in administering the plan, minus the investment return on fund assets (or plus negative returns), plus the net cost to the company of losing the use of such funds in the company's operations, or the net cost to the company of borrowing money to pay required contributions. Actual pension costs will *not* coincide with actuarially computed costs, and the two may differ greatly.

Pension liabilities: The sum of the obligations to pay stipulated benefits to plan participants over the life of the plan. The nature and measure of such liabilities were a major subject of discussion in this book.

Pension plan: A systematic way of providing retirement income. Pension plans differ from other kinds of retirement plans (e.g., profit sharing plans, variable annuity plans, savings plans and deferred compensation plans) in that retirement benefits are defined by specified formulas (which relate benefits to such variables as length of employment, average or terminal compensation, and employment category). Retirement benefits are almost always paid out of funds accumulated through annual contributions and investment return on the funds accumulated rather than paid as current expenses of the plan-sponsoring organization. Pension plans may be public (namely, that provided by the U.S. social security system), civil service (for employees of federal, state, and local governments and for career military personnel) or private (for employees of profit-seeking organizations and nonprofit organizations, such as churches). Private pension plans may be either insured or noninsured. In insured plans, benefits, in stipulated amounts, are paid to retired employees by an insurance company to which the employer has paid stipulated premiums (or has made lump-sum payments—that is, bought annuities) for particular employees. In uninsured pension plans, insurance companies are not involved. Instead, the assurance that the provisions of the plan will be fulfilled is made the responsibilities of trustees (hence the designation "trusteed plans" for uninsured plans). This book is concerned primarily with uninsured, therefore trusteed, pension plans of profit-seeking companies. The term "pension plan," without further qualification, will mean just such plans.

Pension-sponsoring organization: A company, or other organization, which establishes a pension plan, and supplies all or most of the required funding.

Present value: The current dollar value of benefits or other payments receivable in the future. That value is determined by discounting the future amounts at a predetermined rate, a pure interest rate alone, or one combined with a discount for various kinds of risk.

Turnover rate: The rates at which a firm's employees, and their several categories, are fired, quit, or otherwise terminate their employment, thus limiting their eligibility for benefits under the firm's pension plan.

Unfunded benefits: That portion of total pension obligations not covered by accumulated pension funds.

Unfunded vested benefits: That portion of liabilities for fulfilling vested benefits not covered by accumulated pension funds.

Vested benefits: Those pension benefits, claims to which are inalienable, under terms of particular pension plans and, since enactment of ERISA, under provisions of that law.

Index

Index

147